A LONG HARD JOURNEY

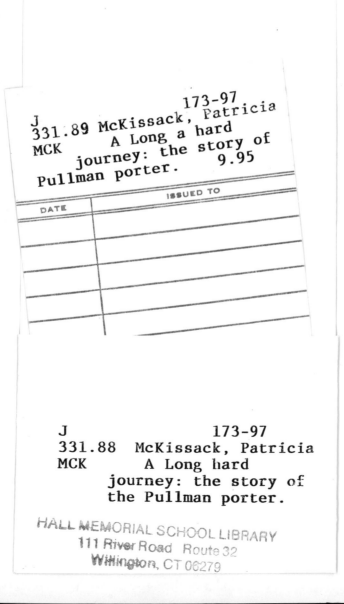

A Long Hard Journey

THE STORY OF THE PULLMAN PORTER

Patricia and Fredrick
· McKissack ·

WALKER AND COMPANY  NEW YORK

First published in the United States of America in 1989
by Walker Publishing Company, Inc.; first paperback edition published in 1995

Published simultaneously in Canada by Thomas Allen & Son
Canada, Limited, Markham, Ontario

Library of Congress Cataloging-in-Publication Data
McKissack, Pat, 1944–
A long hard journey.
(Walker's American history series for young people)
Bibliography: p.
Includes index.
Summary: A chronicle of the first black-controlled union, made up of
Pullman porters, who after years of unfair labor practices staged a battle
against a corporate giant resulting in a "David and Goliath" ending.
1. Porters—United States—History—Juvenile literature.
2. Brotherhood of Sleeping Car Porters—History—Juvenile literature.
3. Pullman Company—History—Juvenile literature. [1. Brotherhood of
Sleeping Car Porters—History. 2. Porters—History.
3. Pullman Company—History] I. McKissack, Frederick.
II. Title.   III. Series.
HD8039.R37U46   1989   331.88′1138522′0973   89-9139
ISBN 0-8027-6884-9—ISBN 0-8027-6885-7 (lib. bdg.)

ISBN 0-8027-7437-7 (paper)

Book design by Sara Reynolds

Printed in the United States of America

2 4 6 8 10 9 7 5 3 1

For Our Son,
John Patrick McKissack
The Bestest

THE SLEEPING CAR PORTER

Fatigued eyes; wrinkled, gnarled hands shine dulled shoes;
seats darkly empty—
passive passengers in their slumberous berths.
Shifting winds jolt the frigid train,
dim lanterns sway....

Defying pain the old porter presses
passengers' clothes with satisfying creases;
in another car a young porter's
curved arms are burdened with unshined shoes.

Winds increase—train rocks
forward blindly against forces
in the black night...metal wheels cry
against the resistance—

"Nighttime seems to never end," the young porter complained;
the old porter continued working...waiting
for the tentative grey of morning—
from separate windows they viewed the blue promise rise,
spirits replenished by distant yellow....

Michele Harnden
1988

CONTENTS

III

The Whole World Smiles with You

1 9 3 5 — 1 9 7 9

INTRODUCTION

Railroading has an unusual number of "firsts," making it difficult to target a single invention, event, or date as the *beginning* of American railroads. The earliest mention of an American-built, steam-propelled carriage was in 1804, developed by a Philadelphian, Oliver Evans. The Mohawk & Hudson Line boasted that in 1826, theirs was the first chartered American railroad. However, in 1825 Colonel John Stevens's steam-powered, rack-rail engine with wooden cogged wheels was the first machine to carry passengers on wooden cogged tracks in the United States. John B. Javis's first use of the steam locomotive in the Western Hemisphere made passenger travel faster and more comfortable and opened the way for the Baltimore & Ohio, the first American chartered passenger line.

As eastern railroads expanded westward toward the Mississippi River, the demand for better overnight accommodations increased. On September 1, 1859, a new chapter in railroad history began when George Mortimer Pullman's first sleeping car made its debut run between Bloomington, Illinois, and Chicago.

The original Pullman car was described as a "primitive thing," but shortly after the Civil War, George Pullman developed a sleeping car that was unrivaled in design and service. Giving each traveler pampered treatment—making him feel special—was the Pullman hallmark. But George Pullman didn't give the personalized service for which his name became synonymous. Thousands of porters helped make the legendary Pullman service a reality.

Beginning in 1867, Pullman staffed his earliest cars with the former genteel servants of the Plantation South. His decision to hire ex-slaves set a business precedent and for nearly a century *all* Pullman porters were black. These emancipated slaves repaid Pullman with loyalty and dedicated service. Grateful for the opportunity to stand proudly beside other working people, the early porters worked willingly and joyfully, graciously receiving passengers, carrying their luggage, making up the berths, serving beverages and food, keeping the guests happy—and all with a smile. These men did their jobs so well they became known as the "Ambassadors of Hospitality."

Seventy years later, the gratitude had worn thin. The new generation of free-born, more informed porters was not satisfied with the Pullman Company's long hours, low wages, and unfair company policies. Their smiles changed to pleas in the beginning, then shouts of protest. Unable to get the powerful Pullman Company to negotiate in good faith, the porters united under the leadership of A. Philip Randolph, and in 1925, against all odds, they formed the first black-controlled union: the Brotherhood of Sleeping Car Porters.

The Brotherhood was the largest representative of black workers in America. It was also the first union admitted to the American Federation of Labor (AFL) as a full member, and the first black union to negotiate a contract with a major corporation.

The porters' struggle for recognition and fair treatment is a classic David-and-Goliath story. A handful of black workers squared off against one of American history's corporate mega-giants and won. When the battle was over and the mighty Pullman Company was forced to recognize the Brotherhood, one of the Pullman executives asked, "How did you do it? We never thought you had a chance." The answer can be found in the remarkable story of the Pullman porters, their environment, their work, their play, and their long, hard journey to victory.

THE
AMBASSADORS
OF HOSPITALITY

1829 — 1900

ONE

Pullman's Folly

Come all ye bold wag'ners
Turn out man by man
That's opposed to the railroad
Or any such plan
'Tis once I made money
By driving my team
But the goods are now hauled
On the railroad by steam

from *Pennsylvania Songs and Legends*
compiled by Howard Frey

In the summer of 1825, a steam engine hissed and rattled its way across wooden tracks, and the "Age of Steam" was born. It was the beginning of an unprecedented era in American industrial growth and development.

From the start, railroading captured the fancy of bankers and bakers alike. But as the introductory song to this chapter indicates, there was some resistance to early railroads. Change never comes easily, especially for those the changes will adversely affect. The great Iron Horses rendered the four-legged breed obsolete, which made the horse-drawn transport companies the first victims of progress.

Others besides those who had businesses to protect resisted

railroad development. Farmers, for example, sometimes lost their land in shady deals arranged by unscrupulous railroad representatives and land speculators. But resistance didn't do much good.

It might have been easier to combat railroad development if locomotives, tracks, and coaches had been the creation of a single genius or the results of one man's labor. But *people* built railroads, and people worked for them, rode them, and depended on them for moving materials and goods. In the introduction to *Workin' On the Railroad*, Richard Reinhardt, the editor, explains the railroad phenomenon best. From 1829 to 1934 ". . . the United States spread from sea to sea, fell apart, pulled itself back together, transformed its deserts into farms and its farms into factories, and closed the curtain on its last frontier; and all the while, the mighty railroad occupied the undisputed center of American public life."

By 1835 the railroads linked most of the large eastern cities, efficiently transporting livestock, raw materials, crops, and goods. Passenger travel, though, remained slow and uncomfortable. An 1840-style passenger car was grimly described as approximately seventy feet long, seating twenty-five to forty passengers. The seats were straight-backed and hard; the bare wooden floors creaked. No toilet facilities, lounges, or food was provided. Consequently, men reportedly urinated out the door, spit on the floor, and relaxed by taking off their shoes and unbuttoning their shirts. In winter the cars were bitterly cold; in summer the cars were insufferably hot and dusty.

Proper women were scandalized by such filthy accommodations and refused to ride a train that didn't have separate cars suitable for a "woman's sensibilities."

Women weren't the only ones who objected to train travel as it existed prior to 1850. The wealthy enjoyed the speed that trains offered, but they wanted comfort also. A few men of means bought very expensive customed-designed railcars manufactured in Birmingham, England. The owners paid a fee to have their private cars attached to a passenger train headed in the direction they wanted to go. On reaching their destination, the car was "sidetracked" until it was time for it to be attached to a returning train.

Even for the rich, such travel luxuries were impractical. For the average working person it was impossible. Passenger lines saw the problem and worked hard at improving their service quality, but nothing came close to matching the exquisitely appointed European parlor cars until George Mortimer Pullman introduced the "sleeping car."

George Pullman wasn't the first to build a sleeping car. There had been earlier experiments on the Cumberland Valley Railroad from Harrisburg to Chambersburg in Pennsylvania, which, in 1836, was an overnight trip. The line serviced miners who came home on weekends.

The all-male sleeping coach was divided into a three-tiered chamber of padded wooden slabs held up by ropes. It was colloquially called "the coffin rack." The car was heated by a wood-burning stove and lighted by candles. There was no bedding: customers were expected to bring their own. To be sure, most of the miners never did. There was no privacy to undress, so sleeping fully clothed with their boots on was common practice.

It isn't surprising that early sleeping cars became the butt of colorful jokes and scathing ridicule. But as frequent fires and accidents occurred, these rolling bunkhouses were viewed as more hazardous than humorous.

In 1850, George Pullman took a ride in one of these crude sleepers and immediately realized the potential for a bold commercial enterprise. Already he was contemplating the idea of a "hotel on wheels," offering travelers the two commodities they wanted most, mobility and comfort.

■ *George Pullman.*

Stanley Buder, a Pullman historian, stated, "Everyone knew that the problem was to build a sleeping car that could be used comfortably day and night. What was lacking was the know-how." George Pullman had the know-how. Having worked as a cabinet-maker, he understood design and style. But more important, he had the confidence to try new ideas.

George Mortimer Pullman was born in Brocton, New York, in 1831. His family was neither rich nor poor, but Pullman grew up believing hard work and thrift were twin virtues. As a young man seeking his fortune, Pullman became interested in railroads. He saw sleeping cars as a unique business opportunity that could make him a very wealthy man, and he stopped at nothing to realize his goals.

By 1858 Pullman had bought and redesigned two coaches from the Chicago, Alton & St. Louis Railroad. It was the convertible hinged seats that would unlock the door to his success.

During the day, the redesigned car looked like any ordinary coach. At night the seat backs were pushed down to form a straight platform over which mattresses were laid. The upper berths were suspended by heavy ropes, with pulleys attached to each of the four corners. These upper berths were pulled up to the ceiling until ready for night use. In addition, Pullman installed toilets at each end of the coach. This was a great improvement over what was being offered by other lines, which were also experimenting in sleeping cars.

Pullman explained the nightly procedure to the conductor who was going to make the inaugural run. After the beds were made, curtains were drawn the length of each sleeping area. Each passenger would be given a blanket; no sheets or pillows were provided. Unimpressed, the Pullman conductor called it "a primitive thing" and complained that he had to "compel the passengers to take off their boots before they got in their berths." Still, the car received high ratings from the passengers and press.

Buoyed by success, Pullman wanted to push ahead with the construction of similar cars, but the Civil War interrupted his plans.

During the first two years of the war, Pullman managed a supply store in Colorado and saved his money for one purpose. In 1863, Pullman returned to Chicago. There he and a friend, Ben Field, pooled their savings in order to build an original sleeping car that would give the general public the same luxurious comfort expected in wealthy homes and the service generally associated with fine hotels.

To many observers the idea seemed silly. They even called the experiment "Pullman's folly." The young train-car builder chose to march to the beat of his own drummer. He hired experienced German craftsmen and sunk $20,170 into constructing the luxury sleeping car called the *Pioneer*. That one coach cost five times what the average passenger car cost in the mid-1860s. But Pullman only used the best materials in his new enterprise.

The *Pioneer* was exceptional, grand in every detail. It had a polished black-walnut interior set off by candled chandeliers, plush seats, and carpeting. Pullman used pure linen bedding and marble washstands, features unheard of in a "public car." Some critics went so far as to suggest that Pullman's accommodations were extravagant and therefore morally corrupt. But the public responded enthusiastically, calling the *Pioneer* "a wonder."

On a more practical level, Pullman had a serious problem to overcome. Railroads balked at his sleeping car design because the *Pioneer* was heavier and wider than standard coaches, making it difficult to run on most railroads. As a result, Pullman's business remained slow until 1865.

Three events gave George Pullman a lucky break: the Emancipation Proclamation of 1863, the death of Abraham Lincoln in 1865, and the completion of the first intercontinental railroad four years later.

Other sleeper-car companies had emerged, but within a few years, overnight passengers showed a preference for the Pullman. The reason was service. George Pullman understood his competitive edge and jealously guarded his company's reputation. He personally guaranteed comfort with unqualified service aboard his sleepers, boasting, "No request is too small or too large for us to handle." Although he maintained control over all Pullman car employees and services, how could he make good his promise? He needed a well-trained, loyal, and responsible staff.

Four million men, women, and children had been freed by Abraham Lincoln in the Emancipation Proclamation of 1863. They were experiencing freedom for the first time, but most were poorly educated and unemployed. It was from among this group of newly freed slaves that George Pullman chose his first porters—the men who would help him build an empire.

It's not clear why Pullman chose to hire ex-slaves. One rumor credited Abraham Lincoln with having asked George Pullman to consider hiring freed blacks. Pullman's daughter dismissed the notion that her father had somehow "created the job for the emancipated slave." To her knowledge, her father had never met the president, and she was "entirely sure the latter had not suggested such employment."

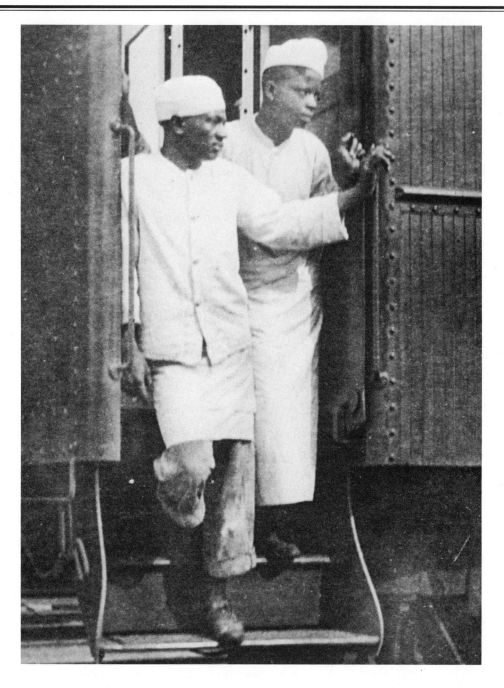

■ *Working on the railroad appealed to former slaves as an alternative to domestic or field work.*

■ *President Abraham Lincoln's funeral car.*

George Pullman was a practical businessman, so it's possible that economics was at the core of his decision. He reasoned that men who had worked long, hard hours for no pay would seize the opportunity to work for pay. Even a small salary would seem adequate.

For whatever reason Pullman decided to use blacks as porters, it proved to be a mutually agreeable arrangement—for a while.

Arthur Dubin, a private collector of railroad memorabilia, stated, "I feel that George Pullman always felt that his break, this accident of Lincoln's death, contributed somehow to the development of his company."

An Illinois State official had once taken a ride in the *Pioneer*, and he had been very impressed with the coach's design and comfort. When President Lincoln was assassinated, the official demanded that the sleeping car be included in Lincoln's funeral train.

■ *In May 1869, at Promontory Point, Utah, the rails of the Union Pacific and Central Pacific Railroads were joined to form a continuous and uninterrupted route from Omaha to San Francisco. The miles of tracks were built by black, Irish, Chinese, and Hispanic laborers much like the railroad work crew above.*

On May 2, 1865, the Chicago & Alton Line from Chicago to Springfield made adjustments in bridges and platforms so the *Pioneer* could be a part of the procession. Such recognition enhanced Pullman's reputation.

But it wasn't until 1869 that Pullman's ideas paid off. The completion of the first intercontinental railroad linked East and West, making coast-to-coast travel faster and easier. Before then a passenger had to take four trains to get from Chicago to New

York, transferring in Cleveland, Ohio; Buffalo, New York; and Albany, New York. The trip from California to New York took even more temerity. The four-week journey began with a steamboat ride down the Pacific Coast to Nicaragua. After a hike across the Central American jungle to the eastern shore, the weary passengers boarded a ship that sailed along the Atlantic Coast to New York.

The Pullman Palace Car Company incorporated in 1867. By 1868 they had produced forty-eight sleeping cars and leased them out to railroad lines all over the country. Although the Pullman car was larger and initially costly, a few railroad lines felt it was worth it just to have the luxury sleeping accommodations for their passengers.

In time, the Pullman coaches set the standard for other railroad car builders. By 1900 all train coaches were the same size as Pullman's.

Railroad companies contracted with Pullman to build the cars and lease them for a mutually agreeable sales percentage. However, the coach would be managed by Pullman employees answerable to Pullman rules and regulations. For two dollars extra per ticket, ordinary people could ride in the luxury afforded to kings and presidents.

When the West opened up, America was on the move, and Pullman was ready to make cross-country trips a pleasure.

Travelin' Men

Lord I hate to hear that lonesome whistle blow.
Lord I hate to hear that lonesome whistle blow.
Lord I'm goin' where the water tastes like wine.
'Cause the water round here tastes like turpentine.
Lord I hate to hear that lonesome whistle blow.
Lord I hate to hear that lonesome whistle blow.
It blows so lonesome and it blows so low.
It blows like it never blowed before.

"Lonesome Whistle"
from *Treasury of Railroad Folklore*
edited by B. A. Botkin and Alvin Harlow

hen George Pullman offered ex-slaves work on board his luxury cars, he got exactly what he bargained for. To men who had just shed their shackles, a railroad job meant unimaginable freedom.

Men in bondage make icons of the symbols that represent their freedom. Trains were such a symbol to the slave. Many a woeful plantation song spoke about train whistles, locomotives, and escape from the day-to-day drudgery of field work.

According to Richard Reinhardt, even white men considered "working on the railroad . . . the most virile, challenging, and exciting career a man could follow."

The early porters were called "Travelin' Men." They were highly respected, even revered by their contemporaries. A young woman considered herself fortunate to be courted by a porter, and with good reason. They were pillars of their community; they made a decent living and had experiences other men only dreamed about. As a popular song of that day indicated, some women preferred a railroad husband over all others.

> *A railroader, a railroader*
> *A railroader for me.*
> *If ever I marry in this wide world,*
> *A railroader's bride I'll be.*

"Besides," said one porter wife, "they knew what was on the other side of the rosebush, so they weren't so easily turned astray. My own husband was always glad to get home after being on the road."

Nineteenth-century porters traveled to faraway places, mingled with wealthy, well-educated whites, and worked in elegant surroundings. In 1867 the *Western World* magazine described the Pullman porter's work environment:

The furniture is of black walnut, handsomely carved and ornamented and upholstered with royal purple velvet plush imported from England expressly for this purpose. The finest Axminster carpets cover the floor. The night curtains for the berths are of heaviest silk; splendid chandeliers are pendent overhead; elegant mirrors grace the walls. Luxurious beds invite repose by night and when made up for the day the cars betray no trace of the eating or sleeping uses to which they can be put. The total cost of each car is $30,000 . . .

Since most of their neighbors had never seen such luxury, the porters formed an almost exclusive brotherhood bonded by their common experiences. It has been said they had more in common with each other than they did with family, friends, and neighbors. Fathers did so well that they encouraged their sons to become porters. Uncles helped nephews, and brothers spoke for brothers.

Porters saw in their travels what most of their neighbors could only dream about. But on a more realistic level, having a steady job allowed them to marry, buy homes, and raise their children with dignity. And although they were not often well-educated, they were articulate spokesmen for education and the general advancement of the race.

Author Jervis Anderson stated that the nineteenth-century porter was seen as "an example of what black men could make of their lives, within the limits of what their situation allowed."

Meanwhile, George Pullman continued to make it possible for ordinary passengers to experience some of the pleasures and privileges generally reserved for the wealthy. His "Hotel Cars" were designed to give passengers the benefits of fine hotel food, service, and a comfortable bed, all on wheels. Pullman later designed and built the dining car which boasted "every variety of meats, vegetables and pastry" that could be "cooked on the cars, according to the best style of culinary art."

The *Delmonico* was the first Pullman dining car, introduced in 1868. All passengers, whether using Pullman sleeping-car arrangements or not, could now eat in the diners. That also meant the hiring of more blacks as waiters, cooks, and stewards—although these positions were not exclusively black, as porter jobs were.

In 1870, the first all-Pullman train, called the *Board of Trade*

■ *Porters worked in surroundings comparable to the finest hotels of the day. Richly furnished lounges, like the one above, were decorated in velvet, brocade, and hand-carved wood.*

Special, made its run from Boston to California. A baggage car contained iceboxes to keep the wines cool and the vegetables fresh. There was even a printing press on board that issued a daily newspaper, the *Trans-Continental*. It is no wonder James Norman Hall, author of *Mutiny on the Bounty*, said, "I can no more conceive of a world without railroads and trains to run on them than I can imagine wishing to live in such a world."

In spite of his plush surroundings, the porter's job was anything but glamorous. He was viewed as a servant. At first these travelin' men didn't mind playing the role George Pullman had cast for them. They wore the mask very well.

Dressed in well-tailored blue uniforms, the Pullman porters adhered to very specific rules of conduct issued by the Pullman

■ *Pullman chefs were known for their exquisite menus, which included Halibut Vin Blanc, Capon Financiere, Apple Fritters Glacé au Kirsch, and Punch Crème de Menthe. In 1900 passengers were treated to these culinary delights for one dollar.*

■ *Pullman passengers were privileged to dine in lavishly designed restaurants on wheels where an elegant meal was served by a well-trained dining staff.*

Company. Although a pleasant "good morning" or "good afternoon" when greeting each boarding passenger was all that was originally required, many porters took the time to learn the names of their regular passengers and greeted them by name—"Good morning, Mr. Smith"—and *always* with a broad smile. After a while, the smile became associated with the porters, but instead of being a natural outgrowth of a pleasant situation, the Pullman Company ordered the porters to smile.

■ *In the beginning, porters proudly performed their duties, greeting passengers and providing service. They were known for their polished manners and poise.*

Many of George Pullman's other rules reflected the social climate of the day. For example, the white conductor was authorized to assist an unaccompanied woman traveler up the boarding steps. If the white conductor was not around, the porter could help the woman aboard, *if* she asked. In those days, a black man putting his hands on a white woman, even with the intent to help, was considered "out of place."

Once the passengers were comfortably seated and their bags were stored, the porter attended to special requests. He might be handing out newspapers, helping a mother with restless children, or pointing out geographic points of interest to first-time travelers or foreign visitors.

The Pullman porter's primary focus was the customer's welfare. He was instructed—and very often tested—to answer all calls promptly and courteously, no matter what time the calls were made.

When it was time to make the beds, the porter was expected to move with speed and agility. The company rule book was precise. According to Nathaniel Hall, a porter, the rule book specified "the proper handling of the linen closet—the proper method of folding and putting away clean linen and blankets, the correct way of stacking laundry bags and dirty, discarded bedding. A sheet, towel, or pillowcase once unfolded cannot be used again, although it may be spotless. Technically, it is dirty and must make a round trip to the laundry before it can reenter the service."

Porters were not allowed to make noise. "Noise was taboo," reported Hall. "And even a soft knock on the top of the berth [was] forbidden. A porter must gently shake the curtains on the bedding from without."

Pullman demanded that all passengers were made to feel special, and part of the Pullman trademark was being waited on by a humble, smiling black servant. Porters' salaries were deliberately kept low so they'd be dependent upon the tip to make ends meet.

The public knew that on a Pullman coach, the customer was always right. No exceptions. But in some cases, travelers took this to its illogical extreme. For example, young college students liked to chide, embarrass, and harass a porter to see how much he would take. It was a foolish game that the porters had no choice but to play. If the porter went along with whatever was required of him, providing laughs at the cost of his self-respect, the students rewarded him with a big tip. Also, a porter was very often the target of cruel practical jokes and insensitive racial slurs. But if he endured it without a word of protest, again he was rewarded for being such a "good sport."

Some passengers resorted to physical abuse: kicking, poking, and shoving. The porter could not speak up for himself, or expect the company to help. In fact the company's inaction regarding the poor treatment of porters was interpreted by the public to mean the men in blue were nonhumans. Taking the lead from Pullman, the public disregarded the porters' feelings and crushed their manhood beneath its heel. Without company protection or job security, the early porters could either bury their pride and quietly accept their circumstances or quit. Some quit, but most had no choice but to stay.

Even under these circumstances, the porters took pride in their work, salvaging their manhood in the respect they received at home. Between 1867 and 1890, the early porters earned a reputation for being outstanding employees, highly praised for their honesty, politeness, and reliability. More than a few white passengers were shocked to learn that porters were "remarkably intelligent."

George Pullman and his "Ambassadors of Hospitality" were highly praised by both races. At the 1893 Chicago World's Fair, Pullman was honored for being the largest employer of former slaves. President Grover Cleveland cited Pullman as an example of how other businesses could use blacks in jobs of "service." Travelers all over the world praised the "smiling porter," who became the role model of the black employee—grinning and satisfied, happy and uncomplaining.

Even Frederick Douglass, renowned black orator, newspaper publisher, and leading abolitionist, praised George Pullman for his hiring practices, and thanked him for being the "best friend of the

■ *The nineteenth-century Pullman porters endeavored to fulfill the company motto: TRAVEL AND SLEEP, SAFETY AND COMFORT IN A PULLMAN.*

black worker." (In later years, the Pullman Company would use Douglass's quote to garner support against union porters.)

Some of those who knew George Pullman privately doubted that he ever befriended anyone. Described as a megalomaniac who abused wealth and power to get what he wanted, his simplistic philosophy was "my rule or your ruin." Other historians claim that Pullman was a "complex man" who was misunderstood.

While historians disagree about Pullman's character, his genius for business was never questioned. From 1869 until his death in 1897, George Mortimer Pullman managed the Pullman Company like a well-oiled machine.

In 1880, Pullman set aside thirty-six hundred acres in the southern outskirts of Chicago and built a planned community called Pullman, Illinois. Twelve thousand white Pullman employees were required to live in the company-owned town. They had to shop at company-owned stores, and even worship in a company-owned church. Black employees were not permitted to live in Pullman.

Rents were high but salaries were low, and many of the employees were actually starving. All living expenses were taken out of each employee's paycheck. One man reportedly earned two cents after all his company debts had been deducted.

White Pullman employees rebelled by unionizing under the leadership of Eugene Debs, a socialist labor leader. Black employees were not invited to participate.

After serving in the Indiana State Legislature, Debs had helped establish and was currently serving as the president of the American Railway Union (ARU). Pullman refused to recognize the ARU and on May 11, 1894, 90 percent of the workers walked off their jobs. The rest of the employees, who were black, were laid off. The company shut down, and the historic Pullman strike was under way. A court ordered the strikers back to work. Debs and the ARU members refused to obey the court order. Police officers were sent to arrest the striking workers.

In July 1894, during a confrontation between the strikers and police officers, violence broke out, and during two dreadful days of rioting, seventeen people were killed and several hundred buildings were burned and looted.

The Chicago press blamed Eugene Debs and the ARU for what happened. Debs was labeled a dangerous radical. He was arrested and imprisoned for refusing to obey the court order.

Public sentiment turned against the labor movement. The Pullman workers were tired and confused, and their families were hungry. Slowly the men returned to the same low-paying jobs. Some money was better than nothing.

Pullman took some of the strikers back, but each one had to sign a pledge promising never to join a union while employed by the Pullman Company. Although porters had not participated in the strike, they were forced to sign the pledge, too.

Losing in the challenge against Pullman destroyed the ARU, and in 1897 it folded. Debs, however, organized the Social Democratic Party and ran for president of the United States five times between 1900 and 1920.

After the strike, George Pullman kept a tight rein on his company. It was said that any mention of unions or workers' rights sent him into a rage. When George Pullman died in 1897, his family covered his grave with tons of reinforced concrete. The family said they feared vandals might desecrate his grave. Ambrose Bierce, an American journalist and writer known for his cutting wit, wrote, "It

THE PULLMAN COMPANY.
OFFICE OF THE PRESIDENT,
CHICAGO.

May 25th, 1905.

My dear Senator Cullom:

I duly received your letter of May 11th in relation to A. J. Phillips of Anna, Illinois. I had one of our blank forms of application sent to him to be filled out and returned to this office, and it turned out, as I thought it might, when I first wrote you about him, that he has passed the maximum age, (he is 57), at which appointments in our car service can be made under a regulation which has been in force for many years, and has always, without exception, been maintained. The situation in other departments is equally unpromising, and I have, therefore, been compelled to write to Mr. Phillips that it would be quite impracticable for us to give him the employment which he seeks.

Thanking you for your attention.

Very sincerely yours,

Robert Todd Lincoln

Hon. S. M. Cullom, U.S.S.,

Washington, D. C.

■ *After George Pullman's death, Robert Todd Lincoln, son of President Abraham Lincoln, became the president of the Pullman Company. As the content of the above letter indicates, George Pullman's authority lived on after his death. The company's rules and regulations were rigidly followed and "without exception . . . maintained."*

is clear the family in their bereavement was making sure he wasn't going to get up and come back."

After Pullman's death, his company continued to grow. By the turn of the twentieth century, Pullman had bought out the Wagner Palace Car Company as well as T. T. Woodruff, Jerome Marbles, and Barney and Smith. The company now had a monopoly on sleeping cars. And every person working on a car that bore Pullman's name was a nonunion worker.

THREE

The Baker Heater League

On a Sunday mornin' it begins to rain,
Round de curve spied a passenger train,
On de pilot lay po' Jimmie Jones.
He's a good ol' porter, but he's dead and gone,
Dead and gone, dead and gone,
Kaze he's been on de Cholly so long.

"Been On the Cholly So Long"
from *Treasury of Railroad Folklore*
edited by B. A. Botkin and Alvin F. Harlow

Porters developed a language and history that grew out of their common experiences. And they shared their experiences from coast to coast, north and south. Singing and telling stories helped to pass the time while waiting for an assignment, and it took the edge off being away from home and their loved ones.

Train stations provided quarters for porters called "porter houses." Sitting around a Baker heater, a large pot-bellied stove, the first porters told tales, jokes, and real-life stories that, in time, developed into a communication network peculiar to themselves. For example, if something happened in New York on Friday, porters in every state would know about it on Sunday. Political news, a good joke, style changes, even a girl's telephone number could be passed from New York to Chicago to Los Angeles, or from Minneapolis to St. Louis to New Orleans. This special brotherhood became known as "The Baker Heater League."

As older porters died or retired, their stories became a part of railroad lore, and their legacy helped to reshape and mold new heroes and legends. Just as lumberjacks created their superhero, Paul Bunyan, and cowboys sang about wily Pecos Bill, railroaders had Casey Jones and John Henry.

John Luther Jones, better known as Casey Jones, was an engineer on Cannonball Number 382. On the evening of April 29, 1900, Casey and his black fireman, Sim Webb, prepared to take the Cannonball from Memphis to Canton. The scheduled engineer was out ill. The train left at 12:50 A.M., an hour and thirty minutes late. Casey was determined to make up the lost time. Through a series of mishaps and miscommunications,

■ *Porter houses were located inside some of the larger terminals. But in small cities, ads like the one above frequently appeared in newspapers. Sometimes entire hotel floors were reserved for railroad workers.*

Casey's train crashed. Although the brave engineer could have jumped to safety, he stayed with the train and saved many lives at the cost of his own. Casey Jones became a railroad hero, and many songs were written about him:

> *Fireman jumped but Casey stayed on;*
> *He was a good engineer, but he's dead and gon'.*

Legend tells us in another song that:

> *When John Henry was a little boy,*
> *He was sitting on his papa's knee;*
> *He was looking down on a piece of steel,*
> *Say's "A steel-drivin' man I'll be, Lord, Lord,*
> *A steel-drivin' man I'll be."*

The real John Henry, believed to be a newly freed slave from North Carolina, joined the West Virginia steel-driving team hired to dig out the Big Bend Tunnel for the C & O Railroad circa 1870. Many stories detail the life and adventures of this two hundred–pound, six-foot man who was so strong he could drive steel with a hammer in each hand. John Henry's death occurred after competing with a steam drill, winning, and then dying.

> *The steam drill set on the right-hand side,*
> *John Henry was on the left.*
> *He said, "I will beat that steam drill down*
> *Or hammer my fool self to death."*

Casey Jones and John Henry belonged to all railroaders, but the Pullman porters had their very own hero in Daddy Joe.

Daddy Joe was a real person, but like most legends, his exploits were greatly exaggerated. One story establishes in legend, if not in fact, that Daddy Joe was the "first Pullman porter." He was said to have stood so tall and to have had large hands so powerful that he could walk flat-footed down the aisle and let the upper berths down on each side.

Whenever a storyteller wanted to make a point about courtesy, honesty, or an outstanding job performance, he used a Daddy Joe story. And a tale about him usually began with: "The most terrific Pullman porter who ever made down a berth was Daddy Joe." Then the teller would tell a story like this one:

Hostile Indians were said to have attacked a train at a water tank. The all-white passengers were terrified. But Daddy Joe, with no regard for Pullman rules or his own safety, climbed on top of the train and spoke to the Indians in their own language. Afterward Daddy Joe threw a Pullman blanket to each member of the attacking party and added a blessing at the end. The Indians let the train pass safely.

Whether he was facing hurricanes, high water, fires, robbers, or Indians, Daddy Joe always masterfully dealt with the situation. Legend has it that he even thwarted one of Jesse James's attempted robberies. Daddy Joe got so many tips from grateful passengers, he was said to be "burdened down with silver and gold."

The first porters, who created Daddy Joe in their own image, were proud of him. He represented the qualities they valued—unquestionable loyalty and dedication to the job.

New railroad employees were always the source of a good laugh, too. This new-brakeman story—or one like it—was a porter house favorite:

It began with a young college graduate who got a yearning to work on the railroad. So, he traded in his suit and tie for the rusty railroad blues. Right away he was hired as a brakeman on the Knox & Lincoln Line. On his first run, the engineer was having a very hard time getting the freight up a steep hill. After getting the train over, the engineer called out, "I was afraid she'd stall and the train would roll backward!"

The new brakeman smiled broadly and assured the engineer. "No chance of that happening," he said, beaming with pride, "because before we started, I went back and set the brakes."

Amid thigh-slapping laughter, another tale would begin with: "Did you hear the story about the flagman?" Of course they'd all heard the story a hundred times. But each teller added or subtracted something until the tale was his own. That's how the tales stayed fresh and original.

Stories involving management were also plentiful. Code names for persons and railroads were used so that if a company informer was around, he would have nothing to report. One such story featured the "penny-wise but pound-foolish" railroad car builder nicknamed Mr. Tightpurse. Everything had to be counted and accounted for in his yard.

According to this tale, Mr. Tightpurse made an unexpected inspection of his train car building plant. He spied a small piece of lumber lying in a throw-away pile. The yard boss saw Mr. Tightpurse pick up the useless piece of lumber. Thinking fast, the yard boss ran up to his employer. "Thank goodness, sir, you found that piece of lumber," he said. "I've had four men looking for it for three days." Mr. Tightpurse smiled. "Good," he said. "We must be ever watchful against waste."

In the early days, tips were always a major concern. The porter needed good tips to supplement his meager salary. So tipping trends and passenger profiles were always a hot subject among the Baker Heater League. It was generally agreed that regular riders—salesmen and businessmen—were the most consistent tippers. They carried less luggage, had fewer requests, and more often than not, they were courteous and well-mannered.

The working class person who took one vacation a year brought along a lot of luggage, but he usually tipped because he wanted to "do it right." Newlyweds were less trouble than any other passengers, and the groom tipped well, especially in front of his bride. The most generous of all tippers, however, were drunks, but they were also the most obnoxious.

Women traveling alone were the lowest tippers and the hardest to please. Actors and actresses, when in front of other people, were sometimes difficult, and they carried an excessive amount of luggage. Wealthy travelers tipped according to the quality of the service if they did the tipping, but if an assistant was in charge of the tipping, it was usually half of whatever had been allotted. The assistant would keep half for himself.

Porters knew how to "read" the passengers, and they could tell whether they had a fast, slow, or soft train. A fast train, sometimes called a fat train, was one that kept the porter busy. It was filled with businessmen and high-tippers, but it was often the most difficult. A slow or soft train was one that was either a short run or not fully loaded. Trips between two rural towns were also considered soft. Older porters were assigned soft trains, but younger porters wanted a fast train because they could earn more tips.

Porters had fun on the trains as well as in the porter houses. It was customary for the more experienced porters to take younger porters under their wings. They taught the "greenhorns" the tricks of the trade and shortcuts, but not without a period of hazing. A favorite trick played on a poor, unsuspecting newcomer was the Christmas ham or turkey caper. Several porters, in the presence of a new man, discussed whether they were going to choose the hams or the turkeys the company was offering as Christmas presents. Naturally, the newcomer wanted to know more about how to get in

■ *It was a custom among porters all over the country to have annual banquets and dances, often at the finer porter house hotels, like the one below, located in Seattle, Washington. Invitations to the porters' balls were coveted.*

on such a deal. As soon as the new porter asked, he was hooked. He was told to stop by the superintendent's office to pick up a certificate that was redeemable at any meat market. The superintendents were in on the joke and added to the hazing, sometimes saying that first-year porters weren't eligible or unmarried porters weren't eligible. It was all done in fun, and rarely was a person hurt by the jokes. (In later years, the white superintendents were excluded from participation in the practical jokes. They used the information to stereotype porters as foolish and stupid. To avoid adding to the negative image, the jokes were kept within the group.)

The porters were a tightly knit group. What they lacked in company support, they got from each other—loyalty and friendship. Like most groups, they developed a language of their own.

Anybody who worked on the lines for a while could tell a "real" railroader, whether he was an engineer, fireman, switchman, cook, conductor, or porter.

For example, the Pullman car was called a *boxcar*, the conductor was called *the Big-O*, and a cook was a *lizard scorcher*. Of course it was a mistake to ever use those names in conversations other than with fellow porters. A fireman wouldn't take kindly to being called a *greaseball*, or an engineer to being called a *hogshead*.

All porters were warned to be on the look-out for *boomers* and hoboes. A boomer was a railroad worker who stayed on a job just long enough to pull one paycheck and then move on, and a hobo was a man who either by choice or circumstances rode the rails illegally. Pullman coaches had such fine reputations, people would try all kinds of tricks to sneak aboard one.

A rookie porter was warned not to expect all hoboes to be wearing a "thousand-mile shirt" (a shirt worn a thousand miles before being laundered).

■ *In railroad slang, cooks were called lizard scorchers.*

An oft-told story shared at porter houses was this one, about a portly gentleman who boarded in St. Louis going to New Orleans. He was so self-assured and spoke so confidently, the conductor was certain the man was "Somebody." The old porter was not impressed. He grew even more suspicious when the conductor called for tickets and the flamboyant passenger said he was a railroad man who had forgotten his pass. The conductor accepted his explanation and hurried on. The porter, however, decided to test the man.

"Sir," he asked later, "would you please give me the time?"

The passenger answered, "It is fifteen minutes after four." Right away, the porter knew the passenger had lied, because a railroad man would have answered "four-fifteen."

Sometimes porters didn't report hoboes. If he got past the "smart white conductor," the hobo had a free ride. Porters also smuggled old newspapers off the train and gave them to neighbors who couldn't afford them. And the stories about porters handing food and firewood out the window to cold, hungry people are plentiful, especially throughout the South. These don't seem like large acts of defiance, but in doing them, the porters were breaking company rules. If discovered, they could have been fired.

By the late 1800s, the old Baker heaters were replaced with more modern heating equipment. The Pullman palace cars were installed with the latest technological advancements. And a new black consciousness was emerging from within the ranks of the porters. The new generation of porters had not been born or raised as slaves, so naturally they had different attitudes. Some were college students working as porters to earn tuition. Others were high school or even college graduates who simply liked being "travelin' men."

Slowly, porter house conversations began to change, too. After the Civil War, Wendell Phillips, an American abolitionist, had stated confidently, "Slavery is dead. . . . We have actually washed color out of the Constitution." True. The slaves had been freed, but their children were still considered second-class citizens—free yet unequal, and the U.S. Constitution was being used to justify it.

To the dismay of the old porters in the Daddy Joe tradition, the porter house talk fests were moving away from comic stories, blues singing, and jokes. Frederick Douglass had died in 1895. The more enlightened participants in the Baker Heater League were now more interested in who would emerge as the new black leader than in a new Daddy Joe story. Their concerns drifted away from who tipped the most to who was running for public office.

All across the country blacks were discussing the implications of Booker T. Washington's "Atlanta Compromise" speech. No doubt porters did, too, for his statement would have a direct impact upon their lives as workingmen. Booker T. Washington was a former slave who started a school for black children in Tuskeegee, Alabama.

Washington had been invited to speak at the Cotton Exposition in Atlanta, Georgia, September 18, 1895. In summary Washington "excused" racial separatism. "The wisest among my race understand that the agitation of questions of social equality is the extremest folly." He suggested that blacks and whites were like the fingers on the hand—separate; but when in times of national interest, they could be like the fist—together.

What Washington said pleased whites but only confused and angered blacks. Washington seemed to be saying black men were not equal to whites, and men like John Hope, a teacher at Roger Williams University, took exception: "If we are not striving for equality," Hope wrote, "in heaven's name, for what are we living?"

The loudest and strongest objection to Washington's "compromise" came from W. E. B. DuBois, then a young black professor at Atlanta University, who said, ". . . so far as Mr. Washington apologizes for injustices, North or South, does not rightly value the privileges and duty of voting, belittles the emasculating effects of

■ *There are countless stories about porters, cooks, and waiters who, at the risk of losing their jobs, handed out food to needy people as they loaded the trains for cross-country departure. Anderson Betts of St. Louis, Missouri, whose father was a Pullman porter, recalled, "My father helped feed a lot of people who were out of work or had too many children to feed. He'd bring home loads of food that the railroad was going to throw away. That's how lots of us black people made it down South . . . helping one another."*

caste distinctions, and opposes the higher training and ambition of our brighter minds—so far as he, the South, or the nation, does this—we must unceasingly and firmly oppose them."

Washington was being hailed "the spokesman for black America." His supporters were rich and powerful and included the Pullman Company. However, the black community was divided between Washington and the young "antagonists" like DuBois, Hope, and William Trotter, a journalist. This schism was even evident among the members of the Baker Heater League.

The older porters took Washington's counsel. They remained silent and avoided confrontation. The younger generation used the porter houses as a gathering place for political discussions. Funny stories seemed callous and insensitive when seventy-eight black men had been lynched in 1896 alone, the same year the Supreme Court ruled that "separate but equal accommodations for blacks were a reasonable use of state police powers."

The porters were the first to witness the repercussions of that Supreme Court decision. Mississippi, Alabama, and South Carolina installed separate waiting rooms, bathrooms, ticket counters, and water fountains in their train terminals. Within five years all southern terminals became segregated. Railroads complied by providing segregated coaches and dining cars below the Mason-Dixon line. Jim Crow train cars were poorly maintained, and Pullman accommodations were denied to blacks in southern states.

There wasn't much to smile about once the porters saw that "separate" accommodations were anything but "equal."

THE
STRUGGLE

1900 - 1934

FOUR

"Let George Do It"

Porter! Porter! Give us more air, will you quick!
Porter! The window, please close!

Yes sir!

Porter! This pillow is as hard as a rock!
Porter! Come give us more clothes!

Yes sir!

Porter! Come here, sire.
Porter! Stay there!

All night the people complain.
We is porters, dandy porters.
We run on the vertibule train.

from the documentary film *Miles of Smiles, Years of Struggle:*
The Untold Story of the Black Pullman Porter

t the turn of the century the porter was waging battles on two fronts—at home and at work. On the home front, porters were victims of negative stereotyping. The communal respect they had once enjoyed was rapidly diminishing. Frequently portrayed as a grinning clown who'd do anything for a tip, the porter became the embodiment of Uncle Tomism. Although most porters were not foolish, it was the public's image of the porter.

On the job, porters were subjected to all kinds of physical and mental abuse. They were forced to work long, hard hours for low wages, and all attempts to redress their grievances were denied by the Pullman Company.

Abuse was quite common. If a porter objected or spoke up to a passenger, he was fired. Forced to depend upon tips to supplement his small salary, the porter was often in a no-win situation. If he wanted a tip, he sometimes had to do demeaning things that went beyond the realm of "good service." Some passengers would ask him to bark like a dog or let someone ride him like a horse. If he refused, he lost the tip, and very often was reported and fired.

Of all the indignities porters had to endure, none was more dehumanizing than being called "George," short for "George Pullman's Boy." Porters resented the name and so did the men who were legitimately named George.

The porters' work schedule was long and hard. One Pullman car traveled one hundred thousand miles a year; the porter who worked that car was required to put in four hundred hours a month or clock in eleven thousand miles, whichever was logged first. No overtime was paid unless the porter reached one of these figures. Today, the average work month is two hundred hours.

Pullman rules permitted porters three hours of sleep on the first night out and none on the second and third nights. So, when porters were accused of sleep-walking, it's possible they were. But it didn't help their public image any when they were seen moving about the coach in a semiconscious state.

A returning porter, in from a five-day run, often was scheduled to go back out on the next train. It didn't matter that he wouldn't

■ *Porters worked long, hard hours for low salaries and were inspected regularly for speed, efficiency, and adherence to the Pullman Company manual.*

get to see or visit his family. Sometimes there was hardly time for him to shower and shave, or tidy himself up at the porter house. Yet, if he was caught asleep or untidy, he could be fired or suspended without pay.

A porter was not paid for the time it took to prepare the train for departure or greeting passengers or for the time it took to clean up after a return trip. If a train was scheduled to leave at

■ *Conductors were paid twice as much as porters for doing about half the work.*

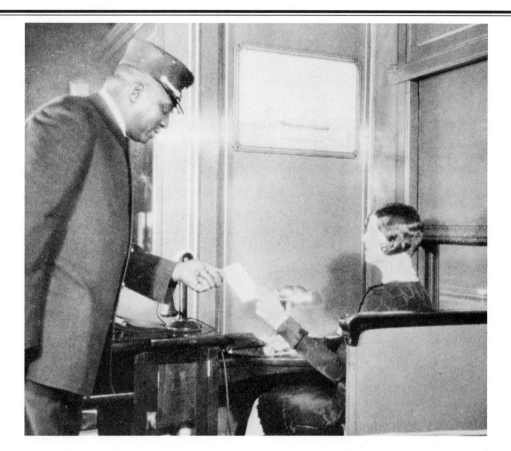

■ *Luxury trains like the Broadway Limited were equipped with hair salon and barber shop, library, and on-board secretary. One of the porter's duties was to serve as a messenger between the secretary and her clients.*

5:00 P.M., the porter reported at noon. If there were no passengers on the train, he made the run anyway (this was called "dead-heading") with the hopes that there would be passengers coming back. An empty train meant no tips.

Running "in charge" meant the porter did the job of the conductor as well as his own. The compensation was only ten dollars attached to his check at the end of the month.

In 1900 Pullman car porters were the lowest paid among railroad workers, yet out of his salary and tips the porter was expected to pay for his own meals while on the road and buy and pay for the cleaning of his own uniforms and equipment. He was expected to polish passengers' shoes, but with polish and buff brushes purchased out of his own pocket. If he was found without polish, he was reported, and that alone was grounds for dismissal.

Pullman records from 1916 show that in one year the company maintained 1,858,178 sheets and 1,403,354 pillow slips valued at nearly two million dollars. Porters were responsible for all linen in their cars. The cost of lost or stolen items was deducted from their salaries.

The United States Commission on Industrial Relations asked a Pullman executive if he felt the porter's salary was enough for a man to do as much as the Pullman Company required. And the answer was, "All I can say is that you can get all the men you require to do the work." That was the sad irony. Black unemployment was so high, even college graduates found that a porter's job was the only one open to them.

Although porters' grievances were myriad, there was no channel through which they could lodge legitimate complaints and there was no organized movement among the porters to start a union.

Since 1894 the Pullman Company had refused to talk with any unions and it was an ironclad company policy that anyone—black or white—"talking union" was automatically fired and blacklisted. The only option an employee had who didn't like working for the Pullman Company was to quit. Pullman had a monopoly on sleeping cars. Where was a sleeping car employee supposed to find other work?

At some point, however, more than a few workers must have talked about their situation. Feeling the human need to regain self-pride and dignity, porters sought ways to change their public image, and whenever they could, they spoke up for themselves. But as the following story illustrates, it was not easy taking a stand against the Pullman Company.

In 1904 the runs to St. Louis were long and hard. The World's Fair and the third Olympic Games were being held there. Double and triple shifts were common. One young porter who had "doubled out" three times was caught sleeping. The conductor reported him to the supervisor, and the porter was fired. A group of his porter friends tried to meet with the superintendent in the St. Louis Pullman office to discuss more reasonable hours and the reinstatement of the fired man. All eleven porters were dismissed on the spot for insubordination.

The fired porters must have thought their efforts were futile. But what they did is significant because it was the first organized "rebellion" within the porters' ranks—a rebellion many of the younger porters took pride in. The older porters, however, scolded the more militant youth for being impatient and ungrateful to the "Company" that had "kept milk on the tables of thousands of black families." And the disastrous results of the 1894 strike and the demise of the ARU and Eugene Debs were a constant reminder to all would-be union organizers.

There wasn't another group action among the porters until 1912. Careful not to use the term "union," porters put together a series of "begging" petitions for a salary raise. Even so, many of the older porters were afraid to sign them. Pullman raised the porters' salaries to forty-six dollars per month, but not because of the petitions. Pullman was getting pressure from white railroad workers who were dissatisfied with their low salaries and poor working conditions, too. Pullman gave a blanket raise to all employees—including the porters—in an effort to offset any union infiltration.

Pressure on the Pullman Company continued. In 1917 a United States Senate committee released a report stating that "the employees of the Pullman Company are unable to improve their conditions through organizations. . . . Workers known to be members of labor unions are promptly discharged. . . . A system of espionage caused black workers to be fearful of affiliating with unions of any sort."

During World War I, President Woodrow Wilson nationalized the railroads, placing them under the United States Railroad Administration directed by William McAdoo. McAdoo recommended that the porters' salaries be raised, and Pullman complied with a one dollar per month pay hike.

When the war ended, the United States Railroad Administration ended, but from the findings and reports gathered by that agency, the Transportation Act of 1920 was passed. And one of the major targets for labor reform was the Pullman Company.

The War Labor Conference Board ruled that Pullman employees had the right "to collective bargaining by representatives of their own choosing, a right that was not to be altered or abridged or interfered with in any manner whatsoever."

The Pullman Company now was forced, by law, to negotiate with unions. The Order of Sleeping Car Conductors organized and Pullman recognized them. The porters were hopeful that they might be included in one of the railroad brotherhoods, but they

■ *Red Caps were responsible for taking passengers' luggage to and from the train at the terminal. At the car, the porters took over the responsibility of helping the passengers aboard and storing their luggage. Like the porters, the Red Caps depended upon tips to supplement their low salaries.*

were denied membership because, at that time, unions were segregated. To stop the porters from forming their own union, the company started the Plan of Employee Representation.

It was organized and supervised by management without porters' consent or input. "What do black men know about setting up a union?" a Pullman representative asked.

Handpicked "company porters" were placed on the board and told which way to vote. But some of the porters were not so easily manipulated, especially Ashley Totten.

Since coming to the United States from the Virgin Islands in 1915, Totten had worked as a Pullman car porter on the New York Central Railroad. He was a steady, dependable worker, cooperative, and well-respected among his peers. The company wagered that having Totten on their team would be a big plus. He was selected by the company to serve as a board member of the company union.

Totten believed that by working within the system changes could be made. But he was dismayed by the company's disregard for justice. The moment he saw that there were more company representatives on the board than porters, Totten knew the proceedings would not be fair.

Many years later, Totten described the first wage conference as a fiasco. The porters' principal demand was for a 240-hour work month. Most of the porters who were there were "from the old school, handpicked by management." One porter even argued against a decrease in hours, saying, "The company is good to us. Show me another corporation that would let us choose our own representatives and pay them besides to fight for their own brother porters."

Totten and other porters who were for the 240-hour work month presented their argument well. They pleaded and begged for consideration, but to no avail. When the argument was brought to a vote, the 240-hour work month was voted down. Only Totten and one other porter voted for it. The meeting ended, but the porters had no victory to feel good about. Their working conditions had not been improved, and they were still earning less than seventeen cents an hour. Totten felt angry and betrayed.

Management reported that the meeting was a success and announced that porters' salaries would be raised to $67.50 per month, from which $2.17 would be deducted to help finance the new Pullman Porter Benefit Association. Whether or not the porter belonged to the Benefit Association, dues were still taken out of his paycheck.

The Pullman Company underestimated Ashley Totten. He knew that if he dared try to organize an independent union, he would be fired, and he knew there would be another "George" to take his place. But Totten figured out that because of the way he voted he was going to be fired soon anyway. So he decided to work for a real porters' union.

Totten returned to New York and secretly met with trusted friends to discuss the disappointing results of the company-union meeting and the possibility of starting an independent union. All their jobs were at stake, because if they were reported they'd be fired on the spot. But if somebody didn't try, the situation would never get better. The idea of getting outside help was discussed, and the name of Asa Philip Randolph was mentioned. Totten knew his background and agreed with the others that Randolph was the man to help them.

FIVE

Freedom from Within

Hold the Fort for we are coming,
Union men be strong.
Side-by-side we're marching on,
'Til victory is won.

Pullman Porter's Union Song

James Randolph, a poor African Methodist Episcopal pastor, married Elizabeth Robinson and they had two children, James, Jr., and Asa, who was born April 15, 1889, in Crescent City, Florida.

Asa's father did not pastor a big church, yet he served his congregation with bold and elegant leadership. Rev. James Randolph loved and respected his parishioners, who were field workers and domestics. But the elder Randolph hardly earned enough to support his family. "My father was poor, but never poor in spirit," the son said, remembering his childhood. "And my mother always prepared good meals and kept us clean."

As the turn of the century approached, segregation and white supremacy spread across the United States. Blacks fled the South, seeking a less restricted life in northern cities. Statistics from that era show that 60,534 blacks lived in Manhattan, but only 14,309 of them were native New Yorkers.

In 1911, Asa Randolph was one of the young black men who fled the South in search of "something better." He was twenty-two when he and his best friend arrived in Harlem, New York. His speech was as sharp and crisp as his features, but his manners reflected the quality of his upbringing. Always courteous, poised, and impeccably neat, he caught the eye of many Harlem social debs.

At that time Harlem was between 128th and 145th streets, and young Randolph saw it all. He joined social and church organizations and mingled with people of all ages. He enjoyed a good discussion and was often the center of a hot debate on a current issue, especially if it had to do with race relations.

Always eager to learn, Randolph attended New York City College, where he took courses in history, philosophy, economics, and public speaking. He was most impressed with his teacher Morris R. Cohen, author of *Faith of a Liberal*. It was while attending college that the young son of a preacher became acquainted with socialist ideas, which appealed to the intellectual youth of the day.

Randolph earned his tuition by holding various unskilled jobs. He learned firsthand what it was like to be treated like a subhuman. Quick to protest, he told his peers that the "jobs offered to black men were neither personally fulfilling nor financially rewarding, therefore they weren't worth keeping." Most times he was fired for "stirring up trouble and making the other workers discontented." During this time he decided his life's work would be helping black laborers better their condition.

Not long after he moved to Harlem, Randolph met Lucille Green, a former school teacher who had graduated from Madame C. J. Walker's cosmetology school. Like Madame Walker, Lucille was also a progressive woman who wasn't shy about expressing her own ideas. She had started her own beauty shop on 135th Street, and it was thriving.

The two had many common interests and shared the same ideas. The young radical was smitten and knew instantly that Lucille was the person he wanted to spend a lifetime adoring. After a brief courtship, they were married in November 1914. For over fifty years, the Randolphs would share many defeats and triumphs, but always together, each one calling the other "Buddy."

Lucille's financial independence allowed her husband to pursue his goals: improving working conditions and living standards for black workers. One of Randolph's biographers, Jervis Anderson, stated, "As they sometimes do about radical zealots, people wondered what Randolph did for a living, for, apparently, he held down no job and had no visible means of support." A friend of the Randolphs said, "It was his wife, of course. She had a good hairdressing business, and she was a sweet and motherly woman. He was lucky to have had a wife like that. Only she could have put up with all those people he used to bring home from political meetings two, three times a week to talk till one, two, three o'clock in the morning." Even Randolph said of his wife, "She carried us."

With his longtime friend Chandler Owen, Randolph began the *Messenger*, a labor newspaper that claimed to be "the only radical Negro Magazine in America, 1917."

At a time when black leaders were calling for "unity of the races in this time of crisis," Randolph and Owen were opposing black involvement in World War I. Unpopular though their positions were, Randolph and Owen refused to sink under the tide of

■ *Asa Philip Randolph, 1925.*

public opinion. They questioned the motives of black leaders who called for black men to defend countrymen who "thought of them as animals without human rights." The young socialist was arrested and branded "the most dangerous Negro in America."

Between 1917 and 1923, Randolph and Owen started more than six political and trade unions. None of them survived—apathy and lack of money or organization being the causes. The *Messenger*, however, experienced some measure of success, but its hardline socialist rhetoric went over most Harlem laborers' heads, appealing more to middle-class intellectuals.

By 1925, socialism had diminished in popularity, but Randolph was still an outspoken advocate of black labor. The porters felt he was the ideal man to help them organize a union. Ashley Totten was sent to make the initial contact.

Forty-one-year-old Totten met the newspaper editor on the street near the *Messenger*'s office. Randolph, the younger of the two men, was impressed with Totten's direct manner and strongly lined face. The tall, well-built man with a Caribbean accent explained that he was a regular reader of the *Messenger* and asked

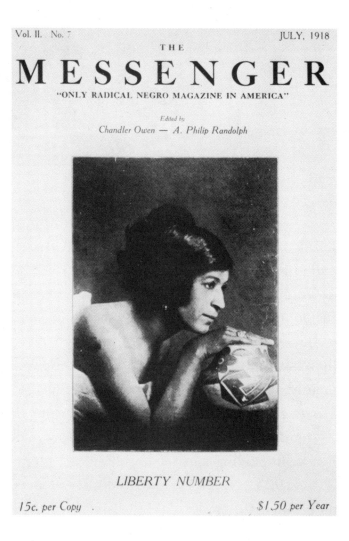

Vol. II. No. 7   JULY, 1918

THE

MESSENGER

"ONLY RADICAL NEGRO MAGAZINE IN AMERICA"

Edited by
Chandler Owen — A. Philip Randolph

LIBERTY NUMBER

15c. per Copy $1.50 per Year

■ *Articles in the* Messenger *helped the porters make their hardships known to the general public.*

if Randolph would speak at the upcoming porters' athletic club meetings.

After researching the background of the porters, Randolph accepted the invitation. His speech before the group was well received. He was an elegant speaker who used the language with confidence. When he stood before the porters' meeting, he looked like a person men would listen to and follow. Self-assured, yet never arrogant, he presented the advantages of a strong labor force.

Immediately following the meeting, the small group of porters met again. They were impressed, and it was agreed that Randolph was the man they needed.

A few weeks later, W. H. DesVerney, one of the older porters, invited Randolph to meet with a few of "the trusted porters" at his home on 139th Street. Porters Roy Lancaster, Thomas T. Patterson, and R. R. Matthews were present at that meeting. Patterson asked Randolph to consider leading them in a fight for a union. The cards were placed on the table. Every previous attempt at unionizing Pullman workers had met with crushing defeat. Eugene Debs's failure in 1894 was still fresh in most labor leaders' minds. "It might take us two or three years to accomplish our goals," one porter speculated. None of the Brotherhood founders had any idea that a twelve-year battle was ahead of them.

Randolph listened courteously, then graciously declined, insisting that he was not the one they needed. He suggested that one among them might be better suited for the job. Although he wasn't a porter, that actually worked to the porters' advantage. He had not been beaten down by the company; he was a man of integrity willing to fight for what he believed; he could not be silenced by having his financial security threatened.

Still, Randolph wouldn't commit, and he left the meeting promising to address their problems in the *Messenger*'s next issue. And he did.

Not one person was surprised, however, when Randolph finally agreed to help. His reason for changing his mind was simple: "It was a job somebody had to do."

On August 25, 1925, the Brotherhood of Sleeping Car Porters was launched in the Harlem Elk Lodge meeting hall at 160 West 129th Street. Five hundred workingmen showed up. Although membership was limited to sleeping car porters, other hotel and office porters attended. Some came just to hear Randolph speak.

Knowing Pullman's hardline policy regarding unions, and realizing that company spies were bound to be in the audience, Randolph decided to run the meeting without any Pullman porter assistance. He gave the invocation, introduced the porters' union song (as it appears in the introduction to this chapter), made the announcements, and introduced the speaker, himself. "At the end of the meeting," Randolph recalled, "I moved the vote of thanks, said the benediction, and told everyone to go home and not hold any discussions on the street corners."

After that Randolph's office housed the Brotherhood, and the *Messenger* became the publishing arm of the porters' union. In every issue the porters' demands were listed:

1. Recognition of the Brotherhood of Sleeping Car Porters as the legitimate porters' union. Abolish the Plan of Employee Representation.
2. An end to tipping and a raise in salary to $150.
3. A basic 240-hour work month.
4. Fair pay for overtime and deadheading.

5. Stop "Doubling Out."
6. Conductor's pay for conductor's work.
7. Institute some kind of pension plan.
8. Four hours sleep on the first night out and six hours on following nights.

The *Messenger* presented the porters' grievances to the public. For example, few knew that porters were made accountable for ashtrays, towels, blankets, and sheets that passengers took as "souvenirs." The replacement costs came directly out of their salaries.

Almost immediately, two hundred porters joined the union. But Randolph knew that the Brotherhood needed to expand if it was going to be a forceful organization capable of making changes. He decided to hold a nationwide membership drive. With a ten-thousand-dollar grant given by the Garland Fund, a supporter of liberal causes, Randolph left for Chicago, St. Louis, and Oakland, California. Outside of New York, these were the three largest Pullman terminals.

The trip had a twofold purpose. First, to gain membership, but second, Randolph was not well known among the porters; his visits would give the men an opportunity to meet and hear him firsthand.

In Chicago, Totten suggested that Randolph contact Milton Price Webster, a thirty-eight-year-old ex-porter. Described as a born leader, Webster enjoyed a good fight, but he liked to win. Webster's story was like many others. He had given Pullman twenty years' service before being fired for "insubordination." One account states that he had forced a passenger to open her luggage so he could remove stolen Pullman property for which he was accountable. The woman insisted that Webster had spitefully placed the stolen goods in her bag. The woman reported Webster to the superintendent, and he was fired. After all, the customer was always right.

Webster was not interested in talking to Randolph, whom he didn't know, or tangling with the Pullman Company, which he knew all too well. He'd pulled his life back to normal and was happy working as a bailiff and dabbling in ward politics on Chicago's South Side. Still, he attended the meeting just to please a friend.

Randolph stood before the three or four men who came to hear him that night. But Webster said later, "The Chief spoke as though the room was filled." Standing there in a blue serge suit and crisp shirt with a starched collar, Randolph talked about workers' rights and job security. "These were terms black men didn't think applied to them." When the new union leader finished speaking, Webster in his usual gruff voice responded, ". . . Count me in."

Before Randolph left Chicago he appointed Webster the assistant general organizer of the national movement, and organizer of the Chicago division. George Price, also an ex-porter, was named secretary-treasurer, and John Mills became chairman of the organizing committee. Randolph's old friend Chandler Owen was part of the committee, too. C. Francis Stratford rounded out the Chicago team when he agreed to be the Brotherhood's attorney.

Webster, who was a take-charge kind of man, was committed to the Brotherhood from the start. As one porter remembered, "Web told the porters he was ready to fight till Hell froze over, and then get a pair of skates and fight on ice."

With the Windy City in capable hands, Randolph's next stop was St. Louis. Randolph was met there by E. J. Bradley, who had already heard about his coming through the porter grapevine.

At thirty, Bradley was balding and his face was heavily lined.

■ *Milton Webster, a pillar of the Brother-hood and head of the Chicago division.*

He was ready to quit his porter job and work for the Brotherhood immediately. Randolph was against it, but Bradley countered that St. Louis was a tough town. One St. Louis porter gave a grim description of the situation: "They had a superintendent down there [St. Louis] who boasted that he whipped niggers. His name was Burr." Bradley maintained that he wasn't afraid of Burr and insisted that he was the only one capable of organizing the union's St. Louis division. The only way to win was to be on the outside. Working porters could be too easily intimidated.

Bradley gave the Pullman Company notice the following day and opened Brotherhood offices at 11 North Jefferson Avenue in the People's Finance Building, Room 208. One week later, Superintendent Burr responded predictably. When he heard that thirty porters had been seen going into the Brotherhood offices, he secured all their names and all were fired. "None but those who had made up their minds to quit Pullman went near Brad's office," said E. J. Bradley's widow, Mattie. "Everybody thought he was foolish for giving up his job. But Brad was determined to see it through."

St. Louis was tough, but if anybody was able, Randolph felt confident that Bradley was the man to do it.

In Oakland, California, Randolph was welcomed by "Dad"

■ *Ashley Totten, a founding father of the Brotherhood of Sleeping Car Porters.*

Moore, a retired porter, who readily agreed to organize a Brotherhood office. By the end of 1926, New York, Chicago, St. Louis, and Oakland were fully functioning divisions of the Brotherhood. Kansas City, Seattle, Minneapolis–St. Paul, Omaha, Wichita, and Boston were added in six months.

Once it was discovered that Totten was talking union, he was provoked into an argument with a supervisor and fired. The reason given in the official dismissal was "insubordination." Totten joined Randolph on the remaining organizational tours. They made a strong team. Totten's speeches were full of emotion; he spoke his brother porters' language, using examples of hardships only another porter could truly understand. They called Totten "the Terrible," a slang expression used much the way "bad" is used today to mean "good." Totten was Terrible, meaning he was Terrific.

Randolph's delivery was deliberate, factual, confident. He used impressive figures and historical facts to support his claims. His language contained motivational words like *self-respect*, *liberty*, *justice*, and *honor*. He was dubbed "the Saint."

Standing before large and small audiences, in city after city, Randolph proclaimed in eloquent speech, "I consider the fight for the Negro masses the greatest service I can render to my people, and the fight alone is my complete compensation." And very often all he got was personal satisfaction.

Sometimes these founding brothers couldn't leave for the next meeting until the members passed the hat to collect money for their fare. In the early spring of 1926, Randolph got word that his mother, Elizabeth, had died. He was in Oakland and didn't even have the money to get home. Lucille and Randolph's brother had to make the funeral arrangements.

There was much at stake in those first two years. If the union was to succeed, it had to have members who paid dues so the work could go on. Randolph, Webster, Totten, Bradley, Dad Moore, and the other funding brothers worked long, hard hours with neither pay nor praise. They believed their union was a symbol of the black laborer's future.

A small group of rebellious black porters had taken on one of the largest, most powerful corporations in the modern world. Randolph believed that by acting with cool determination they would succeed in regaining the self-respect they'd lost so long ago. This message was at the core of every speech he gave. None doubted him.

SIX

The Pullman Company Fights Back

If that wheeler runs me right,
I'll be home tomorrow night,
'Cause I'm nine hundred miles from my home . . .
And when I get you in my sight,
Then I know it'll be alright,
But I'm still so very far away from home . . .

"Nine Hundred Miles from Home"
from *Treasury of Railroad Folklore*
edited by B. A. Botkin and Alvin F. Harlow

To a company as powerful as Pullman, the porters' fledgling union offered no immediate threat. Handling porter rebellions was not considered a top-management concern. The hiring, firing, and daily routine decisions were the responsibilities of district superintendents, and they meted out punishments according to their own whims and personalities. Anybody turned in for union activities was summarily fired. Of course, union participation was never given as the reason. That would have been illegal according to the Railway Labor Act. Some other trumped-up infraction of company rules was listed on the formal records. "Insubordination" was the most commonly given cause for dismissal, followed by "Requested Termination." By using harassment, superintendents forced union porters to quit.

For a while the threat of job termination was enough to impede the Brotherhood's membership drive. But within a year, the plan backfired. Fired porters made excellent organizers, so they were quickly recruited by the Brotherhood. As early as 1925, superintendents began sending the home office notices expressing concern about the growing union membership, but corporate leaders didn't respond.

Eventually top management was shocked when they finally took a look at membership numbers. Corporate's first counterattack, spearheaded by top management, was a highly publicized stock-purchase plan which allowed Pullman employees—porters included—to buy one share of stock at $140, for every $500 they earned. It was a great public relations campaign, but the plan itself was ludicrous. First, the porters barely earned $1,000 a year. How were they supposed to buy stock? And if they had taken advantage of the plan, the company would have used it as evidence that porters' salaries were adequate.

The main office solicited "loyalists" from within the porters' ranks to speak out against the Brotherhood. Some of the more vocal antiunion porters pointed out that their "inclusion" in the stock-option program was a strong statement about Pullman's concern for all employees.

Shortly after the stock-purchase plan, the Pullman Company announced a blanket 8 percent salary raise. Still the porters were earning less than $75 per month, while other employees, who did less work for fewer hours, were paid over $175 per month. The "company porters"—a name given to those loyal to Pullman—

called the raise a major breakthrough in labor-management relations, warning that outside agitators would damage the in-house union's efforts. Brotherhood membership continued to rise.

Management's next tactic was to boost the company's public image, especially in the black community. One sure way of achieving that was to evoke the name of Lincoln. Robert T. Lincoln, the son of the Great Emancipator, was a former president of the Pullman Company, and this was coupled with the fact that Pullman was the first and largest employer of black Americans. Letters were displayed, where porters were sure to see them, from leaders like Booker T. Washington and Frederick Douglass. Washington and Douglass were dead and those letters were over forty years old, written when circumstances were quite different. Where were the company's letters of endorsement from W.E.B. DuBois, Marcus Garvey, William Trotter, James Weldon Johnson, and other responsible leaders of 1926?

The company got a lot of mileage out of a tragedy involving O. J. Daniels, a porter in the tradition of Daddy Joe. He served on the Pullman car named the *Sirocco*, which, ironically, is the name of a hot wind in the Sahara Desert. A recent storm had washed gravel up on the tracks and the engine jumped track at Lackawanna Road near Rockport, New Jersey, killing hundreds of passengers. The *Sirocco* car was pulled parallel to the engine, which was sending out scalding blasts of steam. Daniels braved the hissing steam and closed the door, saving the lives of those on board.

When help arrived, Daniels, who was severely scalded, refused medical attention until a little girl was attended to first. He died before help returned.

The company renamed the *Sirocco* the *Daniels*, the first and only Pullman car named to honor a black man. The company made sure that the black newspapers carried the details of his heroic death. But most of the porters were unimpressed, for they knew that Daniels's widow and children didn't get a pension or compensation for the loss of their husband and father.

Pullman sponsored dances and social programs bringing in speakers handpicked by the company. Randolph fired back that dancing kept the porters' feet busy and their brains idle. In fact, Randolph had an answer to all of Pullman's ploys. "You no longer have the wooden car, no longer have you the typical porter. That porter has passed and a new porter has come into being." And in the *Messenger* Randolph chided company porters, saying that their old-fashioned ideas and customs were holding back progress. "With their slave-thinking they bow and lick the boots of company officials who either feel sorry for them or hate them."

Pullman's public show of porter support was recognized for what it was—a glossing over of the truth. Porters were overworked and the lowest paid members of the working class. Randolph, Webster, and the others addressed the real employee concerns— salaries, pensions, working hours.

Tiring of the game, corporate headquarters reevaluated the company's position and decided to sabotage the leadership of the Brotherhood. If its organizers could be silenced, then the union would fold. Company management soon learned, however, that the Brotherhood leaders were strong, independent men who could not be bought or sold with a cigar and a jug of whiskey.

Surprised that they couldn't shake the leadership, Pullman attacked the Brotherhood's financial resources. They discovered

■ *C. L. Dellums, an outspoken leader in the Brotherhood.*

that the union's main income depended upon the ten-dollar-a-year membership fee collected from each brother. They reasoned that if membership dropped, so would the Brotherhood's income. So Pullman management ordered a second purging in 1926, and hundreds of porters were let go.

By law the company had to give some reason for firing porters other than union involvement. So inspectors were notified to watch for legitimate ways to rid the company of union porters. Even white union conductors worked against the porters.

In fairness to some of the superintendents, inspectors, and conductors, not all of them liked what was going on, and they helped porters as much as they dared. But in 1926, not too many white men were willing to risk their jobs to help a black man keep his.

The mass firings produced the effect the company wanted. Membership dropped drastically. The regional offices were in trouble. But the leaders had been warned, so they were braced for the attack.

Out in Oakland, Dad Moore's monthly eighteen-dollar Pullman "pension" was revoked, and the porter house he managed was shut down. Dad Moore didn't skip a beat. He moved to a new place, put in some used furniture, and kept right on recruiting.

Dad Moore wrote to Webster in Chicago: "I will not stop until the flag of the Brotherhood fly high in the breeze of victory. . . ."

In the Midwest, the porters were afraid to go near a union man. "Brad told me," says Mrs. Bradley, "that every porter that went to one of his meetings was called into the superintendent's office the next morning and chewed out. After taking a tongue-lashing, like a little child, then he was fired. Brad didn't like people having to go through that, so he held all his meetings in secret."

Mass firings and employee intimidation increased and drove the Brotherhood underground. But the company set up a network of spies to report on all union activities. These men (and sometimes women) were called "stool pigeons."

In very strong language, Ashley Totten described a stool pigeon as "a male or female employed as a decoy to spy on others; a confidence man for the dirty work of the employer; a seller of souls; a traitor to little children. In Pullman service, a Negro stool pigeon is a low, degraded human being akin to a contemptible skunk."

Ulas Crowder's story is similar to many retold in later meetings to describe the high level of treachery involved. Porter Crowder was called into the superintendent's office. He had missed his union card out of his wallet, and he was shocked to see it lying on the superintendent's desk. After an interrogation period, the super confronted Crowder with his card, noting that it had been paid up for a whole year in advance. The superintendent gave Crowder a long lecture, warning him about Randolph. He ended by saying, "This is a white man's country, white people run it, will keep running it, and this company will never sit down around the same table with Randolph as long as he's black." Crowder knew his days as a porter were numbered. He was right. Within the month he was fired; the reason: "insubordination."

Wives of porters were an important part of the movement. "I wasn't married to Brad during the struggle," says Mrs. Bradley. "But he always spoke highly of the women who supported their husbands through those dark times. Brad's wife quit him because of his union work. I'd like to think if we'd been married then, I would have stuck right by him."

In Washington, D.C., Rosina Tucker, the wife of porter B. J. Tucker, was very much a part of her husband's work. She helped the Brotherhood by holding meetings in her home, distributing literature, and spreading news. Her husband was protected because she did all this when he was "at work."

Mrs. Tucker explained how their underground system operated. "Now we had a meeting at a certain home once, and the company found out that we had this meeting. So they called the husband in . . . and asked him about it. The porter was able to show by his time sheet that he was out of town. But his wife had held the meeting."

Mrs. Bradley confirms that "it was the company stool pigeons that made it so hard for everybody. Brad used to say the company knew what he was having for dinner before he got home to eat it."

When word reached corporate headquarters that the union was still going strong, a decision was made to go directly to the top. One in-house memo simply stated: "Stop Randolph!"

A smear campaign was unleashed by Pullman against Ran-

■ *Sometimes, to hide the fact that they were holding meetings* for *their husbands, porters' wives took along handicrafts to avoid suspicion. After the Brotherhood was firmly established, the Ladies Auxiliary continued to hold crafts workshops. Prize winners at the 1950 convention were Mrs. Estelle Samuels, New York; Mrs. Maxine Thompson, Los Angeles; and Mrs. Dora M. Jacobs, Hollywood.*

■ *The stress of belonging to the Brotherhood affected the entire family.*
Some marriages did not survive. Those women who endured the
hardships were honored for their courage and strength at the 1950 annual
convention in New York. Left to right: Ella McBride, Denver; Sarah
Harper, New York; Rosina Tucker, Washington, D.C.; Katherine Lassiter,
New York; Elizabeth Craig, Washington, D.C.; and Maisie Sandle,
Washington, D.C.

dolph. The porters were bombarded with literature accusing their
leader of being a "Bolshevik hustler" who was getting rich at their
expense.

Most of the porters knew that Randolph cared very little for
material wealth. He was paying many of the New York office
expenses out of his own pocket, and only taking a very small
salary when it was available. They knew that Randolph had
missed his mother's funeral because he had no money to buy a

ticket home. "Pullman is the only one making money off of our sweat," Webster responded to the allegations.

As one porter told Jervis Anderson, "We needed the support of porters who were financial. Brother Randolph wasn't being supported. Sister Randolph carried him for years. Webster was the most independent, because he was in politics."

Webster was always ready to use whatever resources he had to help Randolph and the Brotherhood. In his eyes the two were inseparable. And Webster understood that if the Brotherhood was to survive, they all had to protect Randolph.

Once the Pullman Company devised a vicious scheme to arrest Randolph in Chicago, for no reason other than to get a picture of him behind bars and then use it to damage his credibility. Webster heard about the plot through the counterspies he had within the company. Webster boarded the train for New York and, using his authority as a bailiff, arrested Randolph first. This way Randolph couldn't be arrested again, because he was already in "custody" of the law.

Much to Pullman's chagrin they were unable to muscle the Brotherhood out of business. Continued attacks only drove the union farther underground, where it became harder to manage because information was less available, less reliable, and more costly. Nothing management did could stop the flow of porters who paid their money in secret, never attended meetings, but sent their wives and others to join.

A few men found the courage to stand up openly for their rights. E. D. Nixon was one of those men. He was a porter from Montgomery, Alabama, and a member of the National Association for the Advancement of Colored People (NAACP). He described himself as a "regular reader of the *Crisis* magazine," edited by W. E. B. DuBois.

Nixon went to a Randolph lecture at the St. Louis Pine Street YWCA. "I heard him talk," remembers Nixon. "He convinced me he knew what he was doing," although Nixon doubted that porters would ever earn the $150 salary Randolph was proposing. Nixon stayed for the entire meeting and put a dollar in the collection plate.

It has been said that the stooges did their jobs so well, if a porter had an argument with his wife in the morning, the superintendent knew of it that night. When Nixon got back to Montgomery, the superintendent approached him about going to a union meeting in St. Louis. Nixon recalls the incident. "I said, yes I did. So he says, 'I'll tell you right now, we ain't going to have none of our porters attending the Brotherhood meeting.' I says, 'Well, if somebody told you I attended the meeting there, maybe they told you also that I joined yesterday.' And before he could answer me, I said, 'Of course, before I joined I thought about what lawyer I wanted to have handle my case if you started to mess with my job. And that's what I'm going to do—I'm going to drag anybody into court that messes with my job.' And I didn't even know a lawyer's name at that time. But I bluffed him out so that he didn't bother me. And from then on I was a strong supporter of A. Philip Randolph."

The Pullman Company refused to recognize Randolph or the Brotherhood of Sleeping Car Porters, insisting that its own Plan of Employee Representation was the union the porters wanted and needed. There were enough "company porters" to agree.

A porter named Bennie Smith was handpicked to serve on the

company union. He was handsome, bright, and soft-spoken. He was just the kind of man they needed in the company union. He was nominated and approved. Little did the company know that Bennie Smith was an underground Brotherhood member. Webster had recruited him, saying, "Two can play the spy game."

Bennie was from the Omaha district, so when he got notification that a big company union meeting was going to be held in Chicago, he called Webster. Porters were pouring in from all over the country for another "wage meeting."

After each session with Pullman, Smith returned to the Vincennes Hotel where he gave Randolph and Webster the scoop. He told them Pullman had refused to discuss pensions, cutting the work month to 240 hours, or any issues regarding working conditions. The agenda had been previously set, and no deviations were accepted.

On the last day, the company offered a small raise on a take-it-or-leave-it basis. The "company men" took it; Bennie couldn't force himself to take it, and refused to sign the wage agreement. The porters' salaries were still less than seventy-five dollars a month. Not long afterward, Smith was harassed and finally fired.

The Brotherhood sent him to Kansas City where he worked with Ashley Totten as an organizer. Then Bennie was sent to Jacksonville, Florida, to set up a Brotherhood office there. A stool pigeon turned him in, and Smith was arrested for preaching social equality in the South. Smith hired a young lawyer, who gave him a quick lesson in 1926 southern justice. More than likely, the young lawyer concluded, Bennie was going to prison and might possibly get hanged "on the way." Smith sent word of his situation to the New York office. Randolph told Smith to get out of Florida as fast as he could. Bennie wanted to stay and fight for justice. Webster sent the next response, and didn't mince words. Wiring Smith the forty-dollar train fare, Webster sent clear instructions: "Get the —— out of there!" After that incident, Bennie Smith was sent to Detroit where he remained throughout the Brotherhood struggle. The South was not unionized until much later. Southern porters joined northern districts.

Those who knew Randolph recognized by late 1926 that he was weary, but the fire in his speech never flickered and his enthusiasm never wavered. Meeting after meeting, Randolph pressed on, speaking to anybody who would listen. With moving compassion he said, "I am undaunted and unafraid. The only reward that I seek is that your cause secures a full and complete vindication. Despite the curses that have been heaped upon my head because I dared to tell the truth, I have no ill feeling against any man. Let us not hate our detractors, for they must be saved with the expansive and redeeming love of the Brotherhood."

Then it was time to move on again . . . another city, another group to convince. But most of the time Randolph was alone on the road, eating on the run, then running for his life. He must have felt, like the hoboes who sang the old road song, "nine hundred miles away from home" and away from his beloved Lucille.

SEVEN

Rockin' the Boat

Sometimes I feel like a motherless child.
Sometimes I feel like a motherless child.
Sometimes I feel like a motherless child.
A long, long way from home.
A long way from home.

Sometimes I feel like I'm almost down.
Sometimes I feel like I'm almost down.
Sometimes I feel like I'm almost down.
A long, long way from home.
A long way from home.

Black American Spiritual

Randolph once remarked that if the Pullman Company paid the porters half of what they spent on sabotaging the union, there would have been no need for him. Randolph was convinced that the company was its own worst enemy. The company left behind a paper trail of memos and letters verifying the intensity with which they fought the Brotherhood. Its strong-arm methods were ineffective against the Brotherhood, but they were successful in dividing the black community.

Unlike the 1960s civil rights movement, the porters in the 1920s were not supported by a black consensus. A porter's job was not one many black leaders were willing to buck the white establishment to defend. Why jeopardize black institutional stability for what they believed was a losing cause? So porters were advised by their friends and neighbors to stop "rockin' the boat."

The black "establishment"—churches, social organizations, politicians, and the black press—stood solidly against the Brotherhood. There were exceptions, but the porters weren't given the kind of overwhelming support their cause required.

The International Brotherhood Protective Order of Elks of the World (IBPOE of W), one of the largest fraternal organizations in the black community, passed a national resolution against unions, saying, ". . . unionism is calculated to do our people all sorts of harm and injure them with the employing class in America . . ." Curiously enough, Randolph was an Elk and a member of Alpha Phi Alpha Fraternity, which had also withheld support. There is no indication that the antiunion opinions were based on anything more than the prevailing attitudes of that time. Since the days of Eugene Debs, unions had been considered nesting grounds for radicals and communist-inspired plots designed to overthrow American democracy. Most black organizations wanted to be accepted as "100 percent American," so they distanced themselves from anybody and anything that might taint their image. Unions headed the list of un-American groups.

But there were some black people, politicians in particular, whose motives were more self-serving. Pullman found a few such characters who, at the company's expense, traveled all over the country speaking out against the Brotherhood.

One politician was reportedly paid four thousand dollars to spread negative rumors about the Brotherhood. Other people were recruited and paid well to raise doubts and plant seeds of discontent. "Why is Randolph, who isn't a porter, heading up the porters' union?" Another point they liked to drag up was Randolph's socialist involvement, subtly suggesting he might be a traitor or communist agent. But correspondence between Randolph and Webster shows without a doubt that both men were vehemently opposed to communism.

In the early days a majority of the black clergy also sided with Pullman. As an institution, the black church was basically leery of unions. So, from the pulpit preachers admonished porters "for biting the hand that feeds you." Although well-intentioned, their counsel only served to hinder progress. Without a union the porters had no chance of getting Pullman to negotiate a decent work and wage contract.

"Usually pastors would allow Brad to hold meetings in their churches," remembers Mrs. Bradley, "but later on, they stopped letting him meet. Oh, our men went through a lot . . . quite a lot."

Randolph countered these arguments as best he could, telling the porters that they were human beings. Being a man of color was not the flip side of inferiority. At work they deserved to be treated like men; in their communities they had a right to their own beliefs; and at home they had the right to be happy. Ideas like that were very radical in 1926.

Early that year, several black newspapers were union advocates, but as Webster noticed, when the "Pullman gravy train" arrived, attitudes changed. The company blatantly bought off the black press and bragged about it in the white press.

Several black-owned newspapers remained loyal to the Brotherhood, among them the *Amsterdam News* in New York. All others were either neutral or opposed it. The Pullman Company helped start a newspaper called the *Pullman Porter Messenger,* close enough to the *Messenger* to be confusing. The Chicago *Whip* was another antiunion tabloid sponsored by Pullman Company lawyers.

Management tried to control what the porters read. They readily provided newspapers that either supported the company or spoke against Randolph or any of the other organizers. In fact, as porters checked in, they were given a newspaper supporting the company's views and *told* to read it.

Most of the information in these papers consisted of lies bordering on slander. One paper accused Randolph of leaving for Russia with seventy-two thousand dollars of Brotherhood funds. He read the article in front of a Denver audience.

The attacks were so well orchestrated, so well financed, and so eroding, Randolph approached the Brotherhood about resigning. They flatly refused his resignation and threw their full support behind him. They believed he was the foundation; if it cracked, the building would crumble. "The Chief," as he was called, pulled himself tall and braced for yet another attack.

The Brotherhood was not without a following. Ordinary people—working men and women, many of whom had never had anybody to speak for them—rallied around the Brotherhood. They became folk heroes. Hotel porters, maids, and janitors came to Brotherhood meetings just to hear the inspirational talks. Many could not afford to give much, but they gave what they had—and like the widow's mite, it was always just enough. Although Randolph was no longer a practicing Christian, he fre-

■ *Porters' wives were very supportive of their husbands' efforts, but none more than Lucille Randolph.* From far left, clockwise: *Milton Webster, Mrs. Randolph, A. Philip Randolph, C. L. Dellums, unknown, Mrs. Bennie Smith, Bennie Smith, E. J. Bradley, and Mrs. Bradley.*

quently quoted from scripture, and to many of his followers he was a Moses figure. Among his staff he was always "Chief."

Bolstered by this grass-roots support, Randolph rededicated himself to the cause and promised never to lose confidence in himself or his staff again. And he never did.

Finally there came a break in the impasse between the company and the Brotherhood. Anderson explained what happened: "Randolph had not appealed to the Railroad Labor Board, which then existed under the Transportation Act of 1920. All railroad unions were dissatisfied with its inability to enforce its decisions, and the big railroad brotherhoods, whose support Randolph was interested in seeking, were then moving to secure a new labor law. While awaiting this, Randolph approached Congressman Emanuel Celler of New York to request a congressional investigation of Pullman's labor policies, and Celler had introduced a resolution calling upon the House's Labor Committee "to investigate the wages, hours, and conditions of the Pullman Company." The resolution died in the Rules Committee, however. The same month, in May, the Watson-Parker bill—supported by the big railroad unions and all railroad managements—was passed as the Railway Labor Act of 1926.

In summary, that meant the railroad workers were protected by law. They had the right to organize without fear. Through the *Messenger*, Randolph got the word out and followed it up with a big membership drive. Porters didn't need to be afraid to join any longer. Brotherhood membership doubled.

The Railway Labor Act also gave the Brotherhood the right to legally seek Pullman acceptance of their union. The smell of victory was intoxicating. The leaders were overjoyed, as telegrams and letters from that period indicate. But their joy was premature.

With the law fully behind him, Randolph was ready for a direct confrontation with the Pullman Company. He began by writing a letter to E. G. Carry, the Pullman president, and as per the Railroad Labor Act he requested a conference, claiming the Brotherhood was the porters' rightful labor representative. Carry didn't reply. Randolph waited ten days, according to law, before sending Carry another letter. Still no reply, but this was not surprising.

Randolph carefully followed procedure, step by step. The next action was to file a complaint with the Mediation Board stating that a dispute existed between the Brotherhood of Sleeping Car Porters and the Pullman Company. He did.

The Mediation Board assigned Edward P. Morrow, a former governor of Kentucky, to investigate the dispute. An inquiry was set up for September 1926. Represented by the best lawyer the Brotherhood budget could buy, the union faced a battery of Pullman corporate lawyers. But Randolph remained cool and confident. The Brotherhood claimed that it represented 53 percent of the estimated 10,875 porters in Pullman's service. In rebuttal, Pullman offered its own statistics based on actual numbers. These figures showed that 85 percent of Pullman's 12,354 porters had voted that the Plan of Employee Representation was the union of their choice.

The meeting was dismissed, although the Brotherhood insisted that the porters had been harassed and coerced into voting for the company union. For months afterward Randolph and his key staff worked at getting 1,000 porters to sign statements attesting that Pullman had used pressure to get their votes on the company plan.

Meanwhile, weeks passed. When Randolph had not heard anything from the Mediation Board in six months, he got nervous and anxious. He wondered what might be causing the delay. That's when he made a costly mistake.

Feeling certain that the Brotherhood was going to win, Randolph decided to begin mending the relationship with Pullman. In June 1927, Randolph sent a letter to Carry stating that the porter the Brotherhood wanted to represent would be an outstanding employee, one who could do his job well and with pride. "You will find the Brotherhood ever ready to fully cooperate with you, frankly, intelligently, loyally, and honorably to achieve this end, mutually beneficial to the property and human elements of the Pullman industry."

Was this the same man who frequently said, "Brotherhood members are a crucial challenge to the Nordic creed of white superiority, for only white men are supposed to organize for power, for justice, and for freedom"?

The letter's conciliatory tone sent the wrong message. Pullman executives interpreted it as a sign of weakness. Randolph had no way of knowing that the company had been ready to concede. After his letter arrived, one lawyer advised the company to "call his bluff."

The general manager wrote Morrow a letter stating that the company had an agreement with the porters which fully met the specifications of the Railway Labor Act. In conclusion, the letter said that "no dispute, and therefore no situation requiring mediation, exists between the Pullman Company and its employees of the classes mentioned. . . ."

A Mediation Board inquiry was held in July, but the Pullman Company sent no representative. Morrow looked at all the evidence and ruled that the Brotherhood did represent a majority of the workers and suggested that Pullman and the union take the dispute into arbitration. An independent arbitrator acts somewhat like a judge, listening to both sides and weighing all the facts and evidence, and then makes a decision both sides agree to accept. But Pullman found a loophole in the act stating that arbitration was not *mandatory*. Knowing that an arbitrator would rule in favor of the Brotherhood, the company refused to cooperate. Pullman held to the "no conflict" position, and flatly denied that the Brotherhood represented the porters. Since Morrow had no power to order Pullman into arbitration, he informed both sides that the Mediation Board had done all that was legally possible to bring about a settlement. Nothing more could be accomplished in the case. It was closed.

Without the support of the federal government, the Brotherhood was left to combat Pullman alone. Randolph agonized over the setback, but he remained positive and upbeat. For the porters it was a bitter disappointment.

Meanwhile anti-Randolph criticism heightened. A scathing article appeared in the St. Louis *Argus* accusing Randolph of insincerity. "It may be that [Randolph] is figuring on getting rich before the porters and maids wake up. The proper thing now for those who have given him money is to demand so much of it back, dismiss him from their case, and try through some other means to get their cause before the proper parties."

Every Brotherhood penny was accounted for, and though Randolph's decisions were not always the best or the wisest, his integrity was never questioned by members of the Brotherhood.

Even so, morale was low and the Brotherhood desperately needed a victory. Randolph decided to make a case about tipping, which he opposed. He'd often said, "We are men who want to be paid like men for a man's work." So, he presented his case before the Interstate Commerce Commission, the federal agency that regulates business transactions across state lines. Tipping, Randolph argued, violated the law because when a passenger paid for a ticket he or she was entitled to full services without having to pay more money.

The commission ruled against Randolph, as he fully expected

it would. But the story was picked up by the white press. It was an interesting headline—Porters versus the Powerful Pullman Company. The *New York Times* became the most outspoken newspaper for the Brotherhood. Favorable editorials helped gain more backing from the white press. Slowly, black newspapers shifted their positions and took a softer tone. The editor of the *Amsterdam News*, a black newspaper, had always championed the Brotherhood's cause; he accused black newspapers of waiting for "white permission" before taking a supportive role.

Even though the Brotherhood was gaining some media support, their fight was far from over.

EIGHT

The Dark
Before the Dawn

Ain't gonna let nobody turn me 'round,
Turn me 'round, turn me 'round.
Ain't gonna let nobody turn me 'round . . .

Black American Spiritual

There is an old adage that says *night is always darkest before the dawn*. Beginning in 1928, the Brotherhood went into a period of darkness that would last nearly nine years. But Randolph was the guiding light, the presence that kept breathing life into the Brotherhood's dying dream. His commitment was so strong, Randolph gave courage to all those around him. Even when his forty-one-year-old brother, James, died of diphtheria, Randolph wouldn't cancel an important meeting, although his grief was intense, as is shown in a letter he wrote to a friend. "I would rather fight a dozen Pullman Companies," Randolph wrote, "than live in a world without my brother." Those around him had no idea of how long and hard he grieved.

In early 1928, Randolph took the Brotherhood's case to the president of the United States, Calvin Coolidge. The president, known to all as "Silent Cal," was a man of few words. Randolph wasn't surprised when, during their visit, he did all the talking while the president nodded occasionally to indicate that he was still listening.

Randolph told President Coolidge about the porters' struggle for basic human rights on the job. He explained that the Brotherhood was the preferred union of the porters, but all attempts to negotiate with the Pullman Company had been blocked. Before the meeting ended, he asked for the president's cooperation.

Randolph and the other black members, who had come to state their concerns about various black American issues, left feeling ambivalent. Coolidge was not necessarily known as a man dedicated to civil rights or labor—in fact, he had come to national recognition as an antiunion mayor of Boston. Randolph believed Coolidge would probably take a neutral position, and he was right. Coolidge didn't do anything to stop progress, but he didn't volunteer help either. It wasn't an encouraging message to report to the brothers.

Not long afterward, the officers of the Brotherhood met to review their successes and setbacks over the past few years. What other legal channels were open to them? They discovered that the Mediation Board could be recalled if there were "any interruptions to commerce or the operation of any carrier." If six thousand porters were to strike, that would be an "interruption" and constitute an "emergency situation."

Webster argued that the porters couldn't survive a strike. Besides, the company made it clear that they would hire any willing worker to fill a job—Mexicans, Japanese, and others. Up to that point, Pullman porters had always been black, but other minorities were being considered.

Randolph agreed with Webster, but quickly pointed out that an actual strike might not be necessary to accomplish their goals. His plan called for a strike vote, which, he explained, was different from an actual strike. When the members voted to strike, all they were doing was giving the union leaders the right to call one. The *threat* might be enough. It had worked before. On the Kansas City-Mexico-Orient Railroad, six hundred employees had taken a strike vote and the Mediation Board had made a recommendation to the president of the United States, who had, in turn, forced the railroad company into negotiations.

When word spread that the Brotherhood was calling for a strike vote, Randolph was approached with a deal. In April 1928, while on his way back to New York from Chicago, Randolph had a layover in Pittsburgh. There, the union leader was met by Robert L. Vann, editor of the Pittsburgh *Courier*. Up until 1928, the *Courier* had favored Randolph and the Brotherhood. Then suddenly, without explanation, the editorials had turned hostile. Randolph knew he wasn't being met by a friend, so he prepared himself for the usual psychological confrontation.

Vann was cordial at first, then he asked Randolph a hypothetical question. Would Randolph resign from the Brotherhood if the Pullman Company agreed to recognize the union and sign an agreement with it? The Chief responded honestly that he would. Vann then revealed that the Pullman Company was willing to talk with the Brotherhood, but they weren't willing to talk as long as a "socialist radical" was in charge.

Later, Vann wired Randolph in New York, saying: "I have authority to say to you that a conference will follow immediately after your resignation is announced. Wire at once."

Randolph wrote to Webster, "I would be willing to make any sacrifice which would advance the cause of the organization." But would his stepping down be in the best interest of the Brotherhood? After carefully weighing all sides, Randolph sent Vann a telegram agreeing to resign, but only if the Pullman Company recognized the Brotherhood first. Vann answered for the company in a *Courier* editorial on April 14, 1928. ". . . Mr. Randolph has been informed that the company will not deal with him because of his history as a socialist. . . ."

Such games were infuriating. As far as the Brotherhood was concerned, the statement was old news warmed over. They went ahead with the strike vote, and a week later, six thousand Brotherhood members voted to strike. Only seventeen voted against it.

Immediately, Randolph and Webster went back to the Mediation Board with their numbers. Six thousand porters threatening to strike established an "interruption of a carrier." Even if Pullman did not agree to meet with them, the Railway Labor Act empowered the president of the United States to establish an emergency board to handle the crisis. Randolph expected there would be some resistance, but he was unprepared for the outcome.

After several months of stalling tactics, the Mediation Board ruled that no emergency existed. In the board's opinion, a porters' strike would not cause a transportation crisis, therefore no recommendation was sent to the president of the United States. The case was closed again.

Randolph was stunned and angry. How could the Mediation Board rule that an emergency existed when six hundred white workers voted to strike? "We are six thousand strong," Randolph said, his voice shaking with emotion. "Where is justice?" But the decision was final. Pullman had won another major battle.

Randolph had gambled and lost, but nobody blamed him. "You need to know," says Mrs. Bradley, "that decision was typical of the times." In black/white conflicts, who was right or wrong was not the issue; everybody expected the white man to win. And the reason was rooted in the fears racism breeds. Simply stated, if the Mediation Board had ruled in favor of an all-black union against a white company, then, in effect, it would have encouraged other black workers to "stir up trouble," and would make them "hard to handle." Eventually, it was feared, the problem would spread beyond the Pullman Company and spill over into society in general. White America would not tolerate a rebellion among its servant class.

The ball was now in the Brotherhood's court. They had voted to strike. Pullman had called their bluff. Everyone wanted to know if the leaders would call for a strike. Webster, Bradley, Dad Moore, Totten waited for instructions. They were ready to follow the Chief. But Randolph hesitated. His confidence had been shaken. Inside he was wrestling with himself. A bad decision would have far-reaching effects on the people who trusted him.

Realizing that he needed advice, the Chief made an appointment with William Green, president of the American Federation of Labor, the AFL. Green and Randolph had worked together before, in 1926, when Randolph had sought affiliation with the AFL. The Brotherhood's application had been blocked by the Hotel and Restaurant Employee's Alliance, which claimed that the porters rightfully belonged under their authority. Porters, in the Alliance's estimation, were not railroad employees but hotel

■ *A. Philip Randolph with William Green, president of the American Federation of Labor (AFL).*

and restaurant workers; the Alliance had used Pullman's "hotels on wheels" advertising slogan to support its claim. Webster and Randolph had rejected the Alliance's offer because the porters would have been placed in a segregated black "auxiliary union." "If we are to be an all-black unit, then we might as well keep our autonomy," said Randolph.

Randolph explained the Brotherhood's predicament to Green, and asked for an opinion. Green's answer was not a pleasant one, but it was an honest assessment of the situation. As he saw it, Pullman had all the advantages—the money to hold out, plenty of strikebreakers, and negative public sentiment. Green reasoned that the country wasn't ready for a black strike. Most people didn't trust unions and strikes were always unpopular, but the idea of black men on strike would seem almost anti-American and might even threaten the security of the black community.

Returning to New York, Randolph told his colleagues that the only way to win a strike against Pullman would be if the public supported them and boycotted the trains. Since that wasn't likely to happen, he moved to cancel the strike. ". . . The strike is merely postponed," Randolph explained, sounding as confident as ever but fooling no one. It was a humiliating defeat, and everybody knew it. "Meanwhile," Randolph continued, "we have forced the company to spend a million dollars to prepare for a strike, thus doing it as much damage as if a strike were actually called." The words sounded good but the meaning was hollow.

Randolph bravely masked his feelings. His public image remained calm and self-assured. But inside he was a troubled man. Negative talk spread uncontrollably through the organization. Membership fell from nearly 7,000 to 771 members, and 300 of those were from the Chicago district. Every divisional office was in debt, and some offices had to close. With no dues there was no operating money. The rents came due. Electricity was cut off. When bills couldn't be paid, the Brotherhood was evicted. Then in the latter part of 1928, the *Messenger* was forced to shut down operations because Randolph could not pay the printing costs. Although Randolph would start up the *Black Worker* a year later, it was never the same.

Milton Webster wouldn't give up in Chicago, although he'd been fired as a bailiff and had lost his political clout. E. J.

Bradley held on in St. Louis, even though his financial situation was desperate. The Oakland district was down to eighty members, but Dad Moore stood firm, promising to "fite to the finish . . . until Deth carry me to my last Restin place."

At around that time, Ashley Totten was horribly beaten in Kansas City. Police reports called it a mugging, but the Brotherhood always believed it was union related. Totten was recalled to New York, where he continued to work alongside Roy Lancaster. Bennie Smith in Detroit was holding on, although he hadn't been paid in weeks.

The group was at a low point, and just right for a takeover. Randolph warned against such attempts. There was plenty of money circulating in the black community, offered by groups whose motives Randolph neither trusted nor approved. For example, when he heard that communists were moving in on the California district, he wrote to Webster, saying, "We cannot temporize with the Communist menace. It's a sinister and destructive crowd which will stop at nothing in order to realize its aim, which is to wreck and ruin every organization which is not Communistic. Instruct Brotherhood men who run into Oakland to denounce and condemn the crowd."

Which is what Dad Moore did. In a letter to Webster he set the record straight about his position. "I was in A meeting with the Communist . . . i got up and said that I was an old man 75 years old and I Dared eny one in the Sity of Oakland or the State of California to say my hands was tainted with half a penny of bad money. And I went for Mr. Randolph for i would stand by my leader if it cost my life. I told them I would die in the street before I would go against my leader."

Such loyalty was heartening, but Randolph knew that the Brotherhood needed more than loyalty to survive. The organization, in its present demoralized condition, could not have withstood a well-planned, well-financed attack from a challenging group.

With this in mind, the Brotherhood leadership decided to reapply for AFL admission in the early months of 1929.

William Green helped push through a policy change that made it possible for the AFL to affiliate with the Brotherhood without having to go through the Alliance. But the Brotherhood lacked the funds and the membership to obtain an international charter, so Green permitted each one of the districts to join independently, and less expensively, under the AFL umbrella.

The move was confusing. Critics of Randolph used the AFL affiliation to undermine him. This time the attacks were not Pullman inspired, but came from other hostile forces who wanted control of the Brotherhood. Randolph was accused of selling out, back-stepping, and soft-pedaling. Hadn't Randolph just written a few years earlier that the AFL was "the most wicked machine for the propagation of race prejudice in the country"?

Randolph had long since stopped trying to answer every charge raised against him. His friends didn't need clarification, and his enemies wouldn't believe him anyway. But Milton Webster always had a ready answer for every Randolph critic. On this issue his quick, no-nonsense retort was, "In America, if we should stay out of everything that's prejudiced, we wouldn't be in anything."

Randolph's strategy worked. The takeover threats and communist infiltrations were minimized by the Brotherhood's affiliation with the AFL. Randolph readily admitted that it was not an ideal situation, but he told all union officials to "talk up the AFL for all it's worth."

Financially, it was the Brotherhood's darkest hour, but it was not Randolph's nature to roll over and die. He would not be turned around, choosing to move forward, always insisting that though the Brotherhood was essentially broke, the union needed to act boldly. So during the summer of 1929, the Brotherhood called for its first national conference.

The handful of members who showed up in Chicago came at their own expense. There they formally elected officers, set up a constitution, and prepared a calendar for the upcoming year. It was an enthusiastic agenda for such a bedraggled group, but far from being a foolish move. Aside from formalizing the organization, the conference helped reestablish their goals, gave them a oneness of purpose, and, most of all, it showed the world, by example, that black people could run an orderly organization and go about business without white approval. With hearts lifted and spirits infused with new life, Randolph sent his brothers home feeling much better than when they had come.

When they departed, promising never to let go or give up, A. Philip Randolph was the BSCP's president; first vice-president was Milton Webster; Ashley Totten, Bennie Smith, S. E. Grain, E. J. Bradley, Paul Caldwell, and C. L. Dellums were the elected vice-presidents; Roy Lancaster was secretary-treasurer.

Dad Moore, who was old and tired, named C. L. Dellums as his successor in California, and supported Dellums for a vice-presidency. Within a few months, Dad Moore was dead. Randolph said of his loyal friend, "We have received no greater inspiration in our lives than from the life and spirit of Dad Moore."

■ *The Brotherhood of Sleeping Car Porters international executive board and officers for 1950.* Left to right, standing: *Bennie Smith, Thomas T. Patterson, G. C. Carron, John C. Mills, A. R. Dailey, Henry Yates, James Bell.* Left to right, seated: *E. J. Bradley, Milton P. Webster, A. Philip Randolph, Ashley Totten, C. L. Dellums.*

Following Randolph's notion that the Brotherhood had to show "evidence of permanency," offices were purchased in Chicago and New York, financed through personal loans. Randolph wanted the Brotherhood to be run like a class-A operation from start to finish. He insisted that their letterhead be placed on the best stationery, and all public talk about the Brotherhood had to be upbeat and positive. "The public does not give much consideration to anything that looks cheap, regardless of its merit. . . ." The Chief stayed positive and ended all his letters on an encouraging note. There is nothing in the correspondence of that time to indicate that the leaders suspected anything but better times ahead.

Then the 1929 stock market crash plummeted the country into one of the most devastating depressions in modern history. Millions of people lost their homes, their savings, and their businesses. Things were bad for everybody, but they were even worse for the Brotherhood.

By 1933, E. J. Bradley had been evicted from his headquarters. He had lost his wife, his home, and his car. Living with his daughter for a while, he did business out of his back pocket. "At that time, hunting wasn't a sport for Brad," says Mrs. Bradley, pointing to her late husband's gun trophies. "He had to hunt to eat." When Randolph told him to shut down the St. Louis office, Bradley refused. Later the Brotherhood would call him "the noblest Roman of them all."

The New York offices weren't doing much better. They couldn't keep the mortgage payments up on the new headquarters on West 136th Street, so the Brotherhood was evicted. The office furniture and records were thrown into the street.

"I picked up the pieces," recalled Benjamin McLaurin, "and moved into an apartment on 140th Street. . . . We went from house to house holding rent parties to pay the rent and buy food." Since they couldn't afford a secretary, every man had to do his own typing, in addition to cooking and cleaning. For two years the headquarters existed from day to day, nobody really knowing what the next day would bring.

Years later, the founding brothers would reflect on those days. In retrospect some of the stories seemed humorous; others remained heartbreaking even with the distance of time.

One Christmas Eve, Ashley Totten didn't have enough money to get home to his wife and children in Queens. He and a fellow brother slept in the office, huddled beneath their coats on a newspaper mattress. Totten wept for the first time since he was a child.

R. R. Matthews pawned his gold watch to help the Brotherhood in an emergency. Thomas Patterson voluntarily doubled out between Chicago and St. Louis and used the extra income to help more needy brothers.

Even Randolph was showing signs of fatigue. But in his usual stoic manner, he suffered in private. If he had a need, it was never mentioned.

Randolph had always taken such pride in his personal appearance, but in those days he wore shoes with holes in them and his blue serge suit was shiny slick and threadbare. C. L. Dellums remembered when Randolph came to California during that time. "He came out sometimes with just his fare, one way. He had nothing else. He did not even have a change of socks or underwear. Sometimes he would sleep at my house, and my wife would look around for his socks and underwear to wash, and she couldn't find any. Later on, when she went into the bathroom, she would see his socks and underwear all washed and hanging up to dry."

Randolph had long since stopped receiving a salary from the Brotherhood. If it hadn't been for Lucille's business and her unfailing love, he might not have survived the ordeal.

It was common knowledge that Randolph had plenty of opportunities to walk away from the Brotherhood. Nobody would have thought less of him if he had. His good friend Fiorello LaGuardia had just been elected mayor of New York. He offered Randolph a city government job earning seven thousand dollars a year. Randolph would not be turned around. "I will stay with my brothers," he said. This kind of courageous leadership helped shift public opinion. People began sending dimes and quarters to help support the Brotherhood's cause. To young people growing up during the Depression, Randolph and the Brotherhood were heroes. Even their strongest enemies could not criticize the character of such men.

It was hard to imagine the dawn when it was so dark. But light has a way of penetrating even the darkest corner. One day a messenger delivered a letter to the Brotherhood office. Inside was

■ *1950 marked the twenty-fifth anniversary of the Brotherhood. There was a large celebration in New York, where a parade, banquets, receptions, awards, and presentations were held.* Left to right: *M. M. Coleman, John C. Mills, Ashley Totten, A. Philip Randolph, William H. Bowe, D. LaRoche, J. L. Reynolds, H. A. Rock.*

a ten-thousand-dollar Pullman Company check. Randolph thought the Pullman Company had written them off. Brothers who were in the office that day reported later that the Chief smiled, then calmly and without reservation wrote, "I am not for sale," and returned the check in the next post. It was not in his possession twenty-four hours.

As his reconciliation letter had changed the company's strategy years earlier, so did Pullman's bribery check. Why they really sent the check is unknown. It is obvious they didn't know how bad the situation really was. Whether he was grasping for straws or totally convinced, Randolph believed the Pullman Company still considered the Brotherhood a threat. Why else would they still be trying to bait him? It was the turning point in the struggle. He squared his shoulders and dug in, stubbornly refusing to give up.

When word spread that Randolph had turned down a "fortune," people wondered if he was a saint or just plain mad. It didn't matter. By that time, everybody knew that A. Philip Randolph and the Brotherhood stood for something much older and stronger than money. And there was no earthly force that could make them give up.

THE
WHOLE WORLD SMILES
WITH YOU

1 9 3 5 — 1 9 7 9

NINE

Just Keep Smilin'

I been 'buked and I been scorned.
Oh, I been 'buked and I been scorned.
I been talked about sho' is you born.

Ain't gwine lay my burdens down.
No, ain't gwine lay my burdens down.
Ain't gwine lay my burdens down.

Black American Spiritual

In 1934 the all-white Order of Sleeping Car Conductors tried to get jurisdiction over the porters. Toughened by years of adversity, Randolph refused, saying, "We will not submit to this. If necessary we will withdraw our affiliation with the AFL and become an independent union again." Randolph knew he spoke the sentiments of all the Brotherhood leaders. They had worked too long and hard to surrender their autonomy within the AFL.

William Green understood and interceded on behalf of the Brotherhood. Although he admired and respected Randolph, Green also feared the AFL would be made responsible if the Brotherhood failed. He knew, if others didn't, what shape the Brotherhood was in.

Then, Randolph shocked even his strongest supporters when he used all the money they had left to conduct a daring membership drive. To everyone's surprise, it paid off. Brotherhood membership increased and so did the union's revenue. Afterward, Green announced that the AFL was admitting the Brotherhood of Sleeping Car Porters as full members. The year was 1934. That summer Green traveled to Chicago and presented the charter to the weary warriors: Randolph, Webster, Totten, Bradley, and the other founding brothers. "There wasn't a dry eye in the place," Mrs. Bradley says, recalling her husband's account of that historic meeting. "Brad had lost just about everything, but it had been worth it. He said it was like a big rock had been lifted off his head."

Ashley Totten compared the founders of the Brotherhood to America's founding fathers. "Those of us who have read American history know that when the U.S. finished the War of Revolution the people were ragged, the wives and children were barefoot, the homes had not even windowpanes to keep out the cold; but America had her independence just the same." And so did the Brotherhood of Sleeping Car Porters.

Emotions ran high that day, and with reason. The Brotherhood proudly took its place among the 105 official AFL "international" unions and made history by being the first all-black union to achieve this status.

Randolph addressed the hundreds of cheering well-wishers who had come to celebrate with them. His message was that the Brotherhood had reached a milestone in the American labor movement and their success was but a small step in the continuing fight for equal rights. It was Randolph's proudest moment.

As far as the Pullman Company was concerned, the Brotherhood's acceptance in the AFL changed nothing. Still insisting that the company union was the rightful representative of the porters, Pullman flatly refused to negotiate with the Brotherhood.

But Franklin Roosevelt was now the president of the United States. He was a liberal who declared himself a friend of those hardest hit by the Depression—the working class. In the area of civil rights he let a breath of fresh air breeze through the White House, appointing a woman as the secretary of labor and inviting Mary McLeod Bethune, a black educator, to serve as an adviser in the newly organized youth employment program. Mrs. Roose-

■ *The Brotherhood took a leadership role in the civil rights movement during the 1960s. Here Randolph is a platform guest along with other human rights activists.* Left to right: *Reverend Martin Luther King, Jr.; Randolph; Mrs. Eleanor Roosevelt; and U.S. Congressman from New York, Adam Clayton Powell.*

velt did her part too. Washington's high society was scandalized when the First Lady entertained black men and women at the White House. But America was ready for these changes, and the Roosevelts carried it off with aplomb. Roosevelt's leadership was bold, yet healing and constructive. Blacks trusted him as they had no other president since Lincoln.

Randolph was invited along with other labor leaders to meet with the president. His feelings were different from when he had met with Coolidge. Roosevelt was sharp, quick-witted, and humorous. Randolph believed this president would look more favorably on labor. And, again, he was right.

As a follow-up to that meeting Randolph appeared before a congressional committee to explain how important it was for the porters to come under railroad law. As a result, Congress moved to amend the rail act. Sleeping car porters and dining car employees were written into the Railway Labor Act of 1934 along with all of the other crafts and classes of employees in the railroad industry. The Pullman Company could no longer "bend" the law; it had to recognize the Brotherhood's right to exist.

Motivated by these new developments, the porters' union forced a show-down vote with the company union, from May 27 to June 27, 1935. With federal protection, the porters voted freely, and the Brotherhood won a landslide victory: 8,316 votes were cast for the Brotherhood and 1,422 for the Pullman Porters Protective Association. On July 1 the Mediation Board certified the Brotherhood as the "designated and authorized representatives of the porters of the Pullman Company."

Randolph would not relax or rejoice. They were closer to victory than ever before. The decision was made. The law was behind them. They waited. What would the Pullman Company try next?

Pullman's general manager, L. S. Hungerford, wrote to Randolph agreeing to a meeting. On the morning of July 29, 1935, Randolph, Webster, Bennie Smith, Bradley, Dellums, Patterson, and Clarence Kendrick sat at the negotiating table with the Pullman Company.

There was still plenty to be done. The Brotherhood had forced Pullman to the table, now they had to negotiate an agreement. McLaurin said of that day, "It was terrifying. What did we know about bargaining? We had no experience." But the brothers fought the same hard battle around the table that they had in the streets, stubbornly refusing to concede on basic demands.

Clearly, Pullman management had not given up. Immediately, they started using stalling techniques to prolong the talks, because the amendment to the Railroad Labor Act was being challenged legally. If the amended act should be found unconstitutional, then the porters' vote would be reversed, and the Brotherhood would be back to square one again. Randolph, who had learned a lot during the past ten years, recognized the stall and on October 4, 1935, he and the other Brotherhood negotiators walked out and referred the case back to the Mediation Board.

The board ordered that mediation would begin on January 23, 1936. The company continued to stall, still hoping for a decision on the Railway Labor Act amendment. The company knew long delays worked in its favor. But unlike other times, the brothers did not grow restless. They remained solidly behind their union leaders even when leaks reported that the union was "selling them short." The porters dismissed the rumors as typical company propaganda.

In the spring of 1936, the Supreme Court ruled that the amended Railway Labor Act was constitutional. Pullman had run out of evasive actions. The company had to resume talks in earnest. Sometimes those labor talks went smoothly and sometimes the meetings got heated.

For example, there was a vulgar Pullman executive who cursed excessively and said terrible things to people. Most of the time he was ignored, but one day he and Randolph got into a heated debate. The company man was yelling and swearing, and Randolph, who was never known to use a four-letter word in public, sputtered around looking for an angry word. C. L. Dellums gives this account of what happened next:

"This fellow was cursing, but the Chief didn't use bad language. . . . Finally the Chief couldn't take it any longer and he looked around at me and said, 'C. L., do you want to make an observation?' But I knew what he meant. He meant that this baby needed some cursing now, and the Chief couldn't do it. That was right down my alley. I told this character that Mr. Randolph was a natural born gentleman. Then I got in there with him and we went to it. I think I knew as many curse words as he did."

The meeting broke up afterward, but it changed the way language was used in future meetings. The swearing was curtailed.

In this way, inch by inch, day by day, the Brotherhood chiseled out a workable and agreeable package both labor and management would sign. On August 25, 1937, the twelfth anniversary of the Brotherhood of Sleeping Car Porters, the Pullman Company cleared another hurdle. The first black union signed its first labor contract with a major corporation.

The porters' salaries were raised to $175 per month. Their

hours were reduced from 400 to 240 hours a month, and finally, they had some job security. No porter could be fired without a fair hearing. And if held off his job during an investigation, then exonerated, the porter received compensation for time lost.

Immediately following the contract signing, the Pullman Company issued a statement patting itself on the back and praising Randolph, Webster, and the others for their outstanding leadership. The Brotherhood issued its own news release, stating Randolph's belief that the porters' victory was a battle won for all black men and women who were seeking equality on the job and in the community. He said, "There was no group of Negroes in America who constituted the key to unlocking the door of a nationwide struggle for Negro rights as the porters." And history proved him right.

■ *Brotherhood on parade, New York, 1950.*

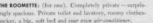
■ *By 1942, the Brotherhood of Sleeping Car Porters was well established.
With better working conditions, porters felt good about providing
service with a genuine smile and giving the extras Pullman boasts
about in this ad.*

Certificate of Service

This is to certify that

CHARLES CLAXTON

has been continuously employed by this company
from   September 1910   to   March 1947   and having
faithfully performed the duties of said employment for a period
of   36   years and   6   months is hereby honorably
relieved from active duty.

The Pullman Company

D A Crawford

PRESIDENT

■ *When Charles Claxton began as a Pullman porter in 1910, he had very few benefits, if any. There was no retirement plan, no job protection or employee rights. By the time Claxton retired in 1947, the Pullman Company had negotiated a full labor contract with the first black union in the United States: The Brotherhood of Sleeping Car Porters.*

According to Mrs. Rosina Tucker, a porter's wife, it would not be "an exaggeration to say that before the Brotherhood championed the case of the porter class of workers, they were only beggars, with hands outstretched for the alms and gifts."

The Brotherhood men were a new kind of employee. The new porters were prouder, happier, and therefore better employees. And the Pullman Company benefited from it.

Besides giving porters better wages, more reasonable hours, and job security, the union also helped with job dignity. Mark

Moore, who began as a porter on the Wabash Railroad in 1948, explained how belonging to a union made a difference to his generation of porters. "I was not a Pullman porter, but a train porter. All porters were taken under the BSCP around 1952. In the days before the union, a conductor could fire a first-run porter if he didn't like him. There was no job security whatsoever."

Standing at his post and receiving his passengers, the mid-century porter had a lot to smile about. But it was a new smile. "There was a difference between grinning and smiling," says Moore. "Grinning meant you were bending and bowing—belittling yourself for a tip. Smiling meant you were confident, friendly, a gentleman. I liked to smile, but grinning was out. Those days were over."

Mrs. Tucker supported Moore when she said, "Yes, the Brotherhood took the porter out of the lap of industrial and public charity and made him a self-respecting worker. It brought, for the first time, sunshine, cheer, and comfort, some luxury and hope into the porter's home for his wife and children."

TEN

I Am the
Darker Brother

We shall overcome.
We shall overcome.
We shall overcome, someday.
Deep in my heart,
I do believe,
We shall overcome, someday.

Black American Spiritual

The Brotherhood continued to advance the civil rights crusade by helping other black laborers.

From the start, women were a part of the Brotherhood. "I was a member of the Ladies Auxiliary," says Mrs. Bradley. "We were responsible for helping porters' female relatives in the area of education, and we also helped keep the porters' story alive."

Historically, the Ladies Auxiliary was formed in 1925 by the porters' wives, but then the group was called the Colored Woman's Economic Council. In 1938 the name was changed, and the group became a legitimate auxiliary of the Brotherhood of Sleeping Car Porters headquartered in New York. "We gave all kinds of wonder-

■ *Each state Ladies Auxiliary unit marched in the Brotherhood's parade.*

■ *One of the Ladies Auxiliary functions was to teach the history of the Brotherhood.*

ful programs, and our outreach to children and families in need was widespread," says Mrs. Bradley.

The Brotherhood also helped to form the Joint Council of Dining Car Employees, now a part of the International Hotel and Restaurant Employees Alliance and International Bartenders' League.

They also helped the Red Caps organize. The Red Caps, forerunners of our present-day Sky Caps, were victims of corpo-

■ *The Ladies Auxiliary also sponsored youth activities. The Young Porters Group was an example of how the Ladies Auxiliary helped teach children to be proud of themselves and their fathers' work and accomplishments.*

rate abuse—long hours, low salaries, and low self-esteem. But in 1938 the International Brotherhood of Red Caps was organized.

The Brotherhood knew the importance of using legal means to support their causes too. At a Colored Locomotive Firemen's Conference, called in Washington, D.C., March 18–19, 1941, the

■ *Pullman car maids were included in the Brotherhood. Here they participate in the 1950 convention parade.*

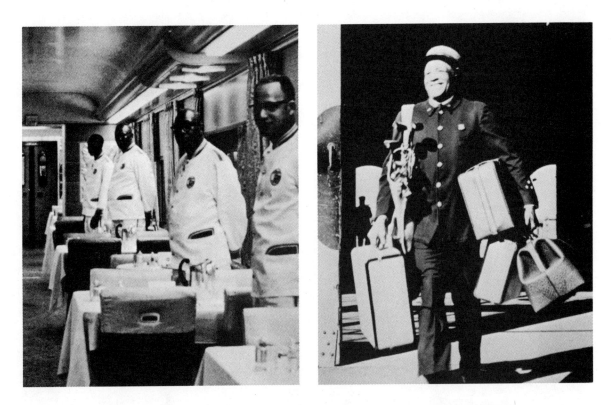

■ *The Brotherhood of Sleeping Car Porters was a role model for other railroad employees. Dining car workers and Red Caps soon unionized.*

Brotherhood formed the Provisional Committee for the Organization of Colored Locomotive Firemen.

The Brotherhood also organized the porters of the Canadian Pacific and the Northern Alberta Railway in 1946.

The list of accomplishments mounted year after year. Randolph and the Brotherhood leaders never seemed to tire in their battle to help black laborers. For instance, blacks were being excluded from jobs in businesses with government contracts. In 1941, with the Brotherhood's backing, Randolph threatened to hold a march on Washington, bringing thousands of black protestors to the

capital. To avoid such a demonstration, President Roosevelt
created the Fair Employment Practices Commission.

The Brotherhood also organized the Committee Against Jim
Crow in Military Service and Training. The fight was against segregated military unions. This group combined with the Brotherhood's Civil Disobedience Committee and worked with President

■ *Brotherhood members, following a reception honoring Randolph in commemoration of the Brotherhood's twenty-fifth anniversary, 1950, hosted by the mayor of New York.*

Harry Truman, who ultimately signed an executive order banning discrimination in the armed services. It was during the Korean Conflict that black and white soldiers fought and died together for the first time since the American Revolution.

All these labor accomplishments reflected the changing attitudes about civil rights in America. After World War II, the

United States was forced to deal with racial discrimination more honestly than ever before. Segregation was an embarrassment that could no longer be tolerated in a democracy.

But the South solidly opposed any kind of desegregation legislation. Southern railroad diners, sleepers, and lounges remained racially divided. Terminals, bus depots, and all public facilities had remained segregated since the early 1900s. Blacks were told to wait . . . things would get better . . . one day. But a younger generation of black men and women were not so willing to wait. Everybody was poised for the incident that would spark a confrontation. It isn't surprising that a sleeping car porter was one of the organizers of the historic Montgomery Bus Boycott, which has been called the "beginning of the modern civil rights movement."

E. D. Nixon had stood his ground against the Pullman Company years earlier when he joined the Brotherhood of Sleeping Car Porters and dared the superintendent to fire him. Nixon was also a member of the National Association for the Advancement of Colored People (NAACP), and he knew the importance of fighting racism through the courts. The local NAACP chapter had been looking for a good test case to challenge Jim Crow public transit laws in court. A tired seamstress getting off from work gave them the case.

Leaving work on December 1, 1955, Mrs. Rosa Parks boarded a bus to go home. When she was asked to give up her seat to a white passenger, she refused, and she was arrested.

Right away, E. D. Nixon, Mrs. Jo Ann Robinson of the Women's Political Council, and local leaders of the NAACP rallied around Mrs. Parks. After Mrs. Parks was released, Nixon and the others decided to call for a bus boycott of all Montgomery buses. Nixon began by calling local pastors, beginning with Rev. Ralph Abernathy. His third or fourth telephone call was to Rev. Dr. Martin Luther King, Jr., the new pastor of Dexter Avenue Baptist Church. He and his wife, Coretta, had recently moved to Montgomery from Boston, where he'd earned his Ph.D. in theology.

Nixon didn't know King well; he had heard through the grapevine that he was a bright young man, a dynamic speaker, and a new father. After explaining the plans for a bus boycott, Nixon asked for King's support. King was unsure at first and asked for a few minutes to think it over.

Meanwhile, Nixon got commitments from eighteen local leaders. When all those on the list had been called, Nixon called King again. Dr. King agreed.

In a television interview, Nixon recalled how he had responded to Dr. King's answer. "I'm glad," Nixon had said, "you decided to go along with me, Reverend King. Your church is the only church right downtown, and I've told eighteen other people to meet at your church this evening at three o'clock, and it would look kind of bad to have that many people coming up to your church for a meeting of this kind and you weren't there."

The meeting was held, and King was elected chairman of the bus boycott. He reluctantly accepted, but with one condition. Building on Mahatma Ghandhi's nonviolent protest for social change in India, King told the boycotters, "There will be no threats and intimidation. Our actions must be guided by the deepest principles of our Christian faith. Love must be our regulating ideal."

After hearing him speak, Nixon was sure Dr. King was a man

destined for greatness. He hadn't heard a man speak with such authority since Randolph.

Montgomery blacks didn't ride public buses for months. The leaders insisted that all segregated barriers had to be torn down before the boycott would end. They were prepared for the eleven months of police harassment and fines. Some of the leaders became frustrated, and the boycotters were exhausted.

Nixon used the story of the Brotherhood's twelve-year struggle against the Pullman Company as an example of how persistence and courage can win over adversity. Nixon was encouraging to others and gave frequent pep talks, the way Randolph had bolstered the brothers during their troubled times.

Meanwhile, Randolph and leaders of other civil rights organizations such as the Urban League and the Congress on Racial Equality (CORE) spoke out in support of the Montgomery Bus Boycott.

Then once again the courts came through on the side of justice. The Supreme Court held that segregation on public buses was illegal. The rest is history. The buses in Montgomery, Alabama, and eventually other southern cities were integrated.

King went to Atlanta to head the Southern Christian Leadership Conference (SCLC) and continued using nonviolent civil protests to desegregate public facilities throughout the South. But it wasn't until the 1963 March on Washington that King became a nationally recognized civil rights leader.

The one hundredth anniversary of the Emancipation Proclamation was coming up in August 1963. In January, Randolph contacted one of his good friends, Bayard Rustin, and proposed a March on Washington for Jobs and Freedom. Rustin contacted the various civil rights organizations and asked for their support.

King's Southern Christian Leadership Conference was included.

The response was overwhelming. On August 28, 1963, more than two hundred thousand people gathered between the Lincoln and Washington monuments. People came from all over the world—sports figures, movie stars, politicians, congressmen, labor leaders, educators. Poor people held hands with rich people. Whites hugged their darker brothers; Jews sang with Christians and employers shared lunch with their employees.

One of the songs that the crowd sang that day was "We Shall Overcome," a labor song from the 1930s. Randolph knew it well, and in his deep baritone voice, he sang for joy.

Randolph served as the master of ceremonies, introducing speaker after speaker. The last person on the long agenda was Dr. Martin Luther King, who delivered a soul-stirring speech in which he envisioned a world free of segregation and racial bigotry. "I have a dream," he said, "that my four little children will one day live in a nation where they will not be judged by the color of their skin but by the content of their character." It was a world A. Philip Randolph had been fighting for, for over sixty years.

It was an amazing climax to a flawless day of American democracy working at its best. Afterward, Dr. King was the undisputed leader of the modern civil rights movement.

When the crowd dispersed, Randolph stood at the podium silent and alone. That day he had passed the mantle to Dr. King. The fight for justice and freedom was in good hands. Randolph, now in his seventies, was tired. "Chief," his good friend Bayard Rustin called, "it's time to go see President Kennedy." And the old warrior turned, smiled, and stepped off the stage.

■ *Asa Philip Randolph.*

EPILOGUE

In 1969 man walked on the moon, A. Philip Randolph turned eighty, and the Pullman Company stopped manufacturing railcars. The airlines had taken the lion's share of the travel industry, and trains were going the way of the dinosaur. The Pullman sleepers were laid to rest in museums. Railroad lines consolidated or went out of business. In 1978, the Brotherhood of Sleeping Car Porters ceased to exist as a separate organization and merged with the larger Brotherhood of Railway and Airline Clerks. Randolph died at the age of ninety in New York on May 16, 1979. It was the end of an era.

ACKNOWLEDGMENTS
CREDITS
BIBLIOGRAPHY
INDEX

ACKNOWLEDGMENTS

Books of this type are not written without help. We would like to thank all those who took the time to find information, share their knowledge, or give an encouraging word. Without such interaction with people this book would have been an impossibility.

Many thanks go to our son, John Patrick McKissack, a student at Northwestern University, who made telephone calls and numerous trips to the Chicago Historical Society and searched the Newberry Collection, tracking down pictures and information for us. In addition we would like to thank Mrs. Mattie Bradley, widow of C. L. Bradley, a national vice-president of the Brotherhood of Sleeping Car Porters and organizer of its St. Louis division, who opened her files and shared so many personal memories with us.

Other people who deserve recognition for their kindness and consideration include: Mr. Charles Brown in Research and Mr. Mark Cedeck in the Barrington Collection of the Mercantile Library in St. Louis; Mr. Walter Naegle, Director of the A. Philip Randolph Institute in New York; Mr. Thomas Schwartz, curator of the Lincoln Collection, Illinois State Historical Society; and Mr. Mark Dysart at the Brotherhood of Railway and Airline and Steamship Clerks, Freight Handlers and Station Employees, located in Rockville, Maryland. And certainly without the cooperation of Mr. Jim Finley, Mr. Mark Moore, and Mrs. Mae Seay, lifetime family friends, this book would not have been nearly as much fun to write.

Finally, we wish to thank our editors, Reni Roxas and Amy Shields, for giving us the opportunity to write this important book.

NOTE: In March 1989, the tenth anniversary of Randolph's death, the United States Post Office issued a commemorative stamp honoring A. Philip Randolph and the Pullman Car Porters.

CREDITS

Pages 64, 71, 74, 75, 84, 95, 100, 103, 113, 118, 119, 120, 122: Mrs. E. J. Bradley, Private Collection; Pages 109, 128: A. Philip Randolph Institute; Pages 11, 26 (both photos): The Illinois State Historical Society; Pages 10 (#24250), 18 (#54402), 20 (#24858), 36 (#73643), 51 (#28460), 121 (#24249): The Oregon Historical Society; Page 6: The Newberry Library; Pages 29, 34: Washington State Historical Society; Pages 39, 47: The Penn Central Corporation; Pages 17, 19, 23, 46: The Southern Pacific Transportation Company; Pages 12, 45: Union Pacific Systems.

BIBLIOGRAPHY

BOOKS

Allen Geoffrey Freeman. *Luxury Trains of the World*. New York: Everest House Publishers, 1979.

Anderson, Jervis. *A. Philip Randolph, A Biographical Portrait*. New York: Harcourt Brace Jovanovich, Inc., 1973.

Beebe, Lucius. *Mr. Pullman's Elegant Palace Car*. Garden City, New York: Doubleday and Company, Inc., 1961.

Bennett, Lerone, Jr. *Before the Mayflower—A History of Black America*. Chicago: Johnson Publishing Company, 1987.

Botkin, B. A., and Alvin F. Harlow. *A Treasury of Railroad Folklore*. New York: Crown Publishers, Inc., 1953.

Brazeal, B. R. *The Brotherhood of Sleeping Car Porters*. New York: Harper and Brothers, 1946.

Buder, Stanley. *Pullman: An Experiment in Industrial Order and Community Planning*. New York: Oxford University Press, 1967.

Combs, Barry B. *Westward to Promontory: Building the Union Pacific Across the Plains and Mountains*. Palo Alto, California: American West Publishing Company, 1969.

Davis, Daniel S. *Mr. Black Labor, The Story of A. Philip Randolph, Father of the Civil Rights Movement*. New York: E. P. Dutton and Company, Inc., 1972.

Hamilton, Virginia. *The Writings of W.E.B. DuBois*. New York: T. Y. Crowell Company, 1975.

Haskins, James. *Revolutionaries: Agents of Change*. New York: J. B. Lippincott Company, 1971.

Lindsey, Almont. *The Pullman Strike*. Chicago: University of Chicago Press, 1963.

McKissack, Patricia. *Martin Luther King, A Man to Remember*. Chicago: Children's Press, 1984.

McKissack, Patricia and Fredrick. *The Civil Rights Movement in America from 1865 to the Present.* Chicago: Children's Press, 1987.

McKissack, Patricia. *Paul Laurence Dunbar, A Poet to Remember.* Chicago: Children's Press, 1985.

Reinhardt, Richard. *Workin' On the Railroad.* Palo Alto, California: American West Publishing Company, 1970.

Simmons, Gloria M., and Helene D. Hutchinson. *Black Culture—Reading and Writing Black.* New York: Holt Rinehart and Winston, Inc., 1972.

ARTICLES, PAMPHLETS, PAPERS, AND SCRIPTS

"John Henry: The Legendary Laborer Really Lived," *The Laborer:* page 9–14, February 1973.

"John Henry: Man or Myth?" A Community Project of Hilldale Ruritan Club, Forest Hill, West Virginia.

Souvenir Booklet from the Brotherhood of Sleeping Car Porters Silver Jubilee Anniversary and 7th Biennial Convention, September 1950. (From the files of Mrs. C. L. Bradley)

Pullman Papers, rule books, letters, and other documents, from the Chicago Historical Society, Chicago, Illinois, and the Newberry Library, Chicago, Illinois.

Script from "Miles of Smiles, Years of Struggle: The Untold Story of the Black Pullman Porter" a PBS Special, Produced by Paul Wagner

PERSONAL INTERVIEWS

Mrs. Mattie Bradley, wife of BSCP Vice-President E. J. Bradley, St. Louis, Missouri, October 1988.

Mr. Jim Finley, former Pullman chef, Webster Groves, Missouri, July 1988.

Mr. Mark Moore, Pullman car porter, Webster Groves, Missouri, November 1988.

Mrs. Mae Seay, wife of Pullman chef Ed Samuels, Nashville, Tennessee, November 1988.

INDEX